How to
STOP
Screwing Up

D1310626

How to
STOP
Screwing Up

12 Steps to a
Real Life and
a *Pretty Good Time*

MARTHA WOODROOF

HAMPTON ROADS
PUBLISHING COMPANY, INC.

Cover design by Bookwrights Design

The Twelve Steps are reprinted and adapted with permission of Alcoholics Anonymous World Services, Inc. (A.A.W.S.) Permission to reprint and adapt the Twelve Steps does not mean that A.A.W.S. has reviewed or approved the contents of this publication, or that A.A.W.S. necessarily agrees with the views expressed herein. A.A. is a program of recovery from alcoholism *only*—use of the Twelve Steps in connection with programs and activities which are patterned after A.A., but which address other problems, or in any other non-A.A. context, does not imply otherwise.

Hampton Roads Publishing Company, Inc.
1125 Stoney Ridge Road
Charlottesville, VA 22902

434-296-2772
fax: 434-296-5096
e-mail: hrpc@hrpub.com
www.hrpub.com

If you are unable to order this book from your local
bookseller, you may order directly from the publisher.
Call 1-800-766-8009, toll-free.

Library of Congress Cataloging-in-Publication Data

Woodroof, Martha, 1947-
  How to stop screwing up : when you hit the wall : twelve steps to a real life and a pretty good time / Martha Woodroof.
      p. cm.
   Summary: "Woodroof's account of using the Twelve Steps of Alcoholics Anonymous to deal with her addictions and stop screwing up her life in other ways, as well. Woodroof creates her own Twelve Steps, a workable guide for anyone wishing to replace a bad habit with a good one, without any reliance on public disclosure or the dogma of religion"--Provided by publisher.
   ISBN 978-1-57174-536-1 (5.5 x 8.5 tp : alk. paper)
   1. Habit breaking. 2. Twelve-step programs. I. Title.
   BF337.B74W66 2006
   158--dc22

2006101600
ISBN 978-1-57174-536-1
10 9 8 7 6 5 4 3 2 1
Printed on acid-free paper in the United States

To Lizzie and Charlie

I hope you will not misunderstand what I am going to say.
I am not preaching, and Heaven knows I do not pretend to
be better than anyone else.

—C. S. Lewis, *Mere Christianity*

I am what I am . . .

—Popeye

Contents

Introduction

One of life's perplexing challenges is that most of us have an awfully hard time not doing all kinds of stupid things we know will make us unhappy. We eat too much. We lose our temper too often. We're addicted to all sorts of stimulating stuff. We tell too many fibs. In my days as a poster child for screwups, I binged on alcohol, took too many pills, had a samurai sword for a tongue when I got angry, and lied to myself a lot.

Of course, we've tried to stop doing whatever it is that makes us feel bad. We've sworn to change our ways, and maybe we did, for a while. Yet the urge to screw up always comes back, as though we human beings are compelled to chip away at our peace of mind with some kind of self-destructive behavior.

There are already plenty of books dealing with how to stop smoking, overeating, shopping like there's no tomorrow—with whatever the specific screwy habit is that plagues you. This book is emphatically *not* one of those. Instead, this book is about dealing with the screwy urge *behind* the habit. It lays out a practical application of classic recovery principles, making them accessible to anyone who's doing something they'd like to stop.

Defining the Problem

I define self-destructive behavior as any habit that leeches the joy out of life. We don't begin life with any such habits. Remember all those long, pleasant childhood days? For a lot of us, they were comparatively uncomplicated and happy. Life was about playing, eating, sleeping, and hugging. The hardest thing we faced on an interpersonal level was sharing our toys. We somehow just *got* the business of living. However, when adolescence reared its confusing head, we began to notice that our families weren't perfect, and the world was a complicated place that didn't revolve around serving our specific needs. No wonder that, by the time we grew up, we had emotional baggage.

I remember one of the first times I realized I'd lost the magic straightforwardness of childhood. My first real job was as a teacher's aide in a pilot Head Start class that was the prototype for the entire program. I was Miss Hege in those days. *Miss H-a-a-a-gee* to my students, a couple of dozen African-American energy elves, most of whom seemed never to have had physical access to a white person before.

It was there I met Patricia the Great. Patricia was four years old and all sass. She's still one of my role models. It could be noon on a blazing hot Carolina summer day, but Patricia didn't care how hot it was. She'd hop on one of the few Head Start tricycles and get *down* on the playground, her legs pumping those three wheels 'round and 'round while she shouted "Barefootin'" and danced to her own music from the waist up. I would watch her from the shade and feel this hunger to *be* Patricia, to once again have an uncomplicated connection between my healthy impulses and a healthy output. I didn't want to slog through life feeling quietly desperate. I didn't want to have to make a choice between feeling conflicted or not feeling much at all.

I was not completely un-self-aware, even back then in my untherapized, nineteen-year-old state. I knew those healthy, straightforward childhood impulses were still inside me. The problem seemed to be that the link between those impulses and my actions had somehow broken down. I can see now that, after a certain age, I needed some kind of spiritual connection to maintain the link. But at nineteen I still confused arrogance with independence and believed that, if there were a Higher Power, I was She. I believed I could think my way out of any mess I got into.

By the time I met Patricia the Great, I'd already begun doing things I was uncomfortable with. I was obsessing about food, skipping class, and smoking. In other words, I'd begun developing coping habits that didn't cope with a thing and would become problems themselves over the next couple of decades.

It was one of these coping mechanisms that eventually landed me in a Twelve Step program. People in such programs don't lecture or criticize. Instead, they communicate their experiences, strengths, and hopes with each other. They tell their stories in the hope of helping other people. In this book, I tell the story of how I reconnected with my inner Patricia the Great—how as an adult, I rediscovered a child's intuitive ability to connect with something beyond myself that people commonly refer to as God, and thus rediscovered my ability to be straightforward with myself and the world. I reject the notion that being grown-up means we are condemned to go through life feeling uncomfortable with ourselves—intending to do the right thing, wanting to do the healthy thing, but instead ending up doing something else that's not quite either.

You will want to read this book if you share my hunger to stop acting in ways that bring you discomfort, compel you to be dishonest, or cause outright despair. In other words, read this book if you'd like to feel more at peace with being who you are, in the world as it actually is.

The Twelve Steps for the Rest of Us

The Twelve Steps of Alcoholics Anonymous are a proven way for those of us who keep screwing up to develop a healthy thinking and living process. I came to the Twelve Steps through an addiction, but you certainly don't have to be an addict to benefit from using them.

In my case, alcohol and drug abuse were simply the two stupid habits, among many stupid habits, that forced me to work the Twelve Steps. Looking back, I am absolutely positive that given my tendency to screw up in so many other creative ways, developing those substance abuse problems was the best thing that could have happened to me. Without a couple of addictions to manage, I would've been too independent (or should I say stubborn?) to follow twelve suggestions from anyone about anything.

A Twelve Step program recognizes substance abuse as not only a physical dependency, but also as a disease of the mind that leads to off-kilter thoughts and emotions. In my experience, addiction certainly gave urgency to the situation, but I've found that the same quiet consistency of approach works equally well in dealing with *any* self-destructive thinking that leads to *any* behavior that's making me feel less than peaceful. These days, my life is useful, full of warmth, and grounded in calm. I like it a lot.

It hardly seemed fair to me that such a liberating program should be readily accessible only to people who'd admitted they were addicted to something. When I listened to non-addicted individuals talk about their struggles and screwups, I heard the same litany of confusion and excuses that ran through my head when I was most mystified by my own behavior. It was like listening to myself before I began kicking and screaming my way through the Twelve Steps (see appendix).

I decided someone should write a book outlining a Twelve Step program for anyone and everyone. Then, being distantly related to the Little Red Hen from the children's story, I decided to write that book myself. The chapters ahead each contain an explanation of a single step, the story of my own bumbling slog through that step, suggestions on how you might work it, and questions designed to jumpstart the process.

I invite you to try working these Twelve Steps. The only things you have to lose are your screwups.

TWELVE STEPS FOR DEALING

1. I will accept that my screwups are hurting me and other people, but I am powerless to stop doing them.

2. I will recognize that my brain and willpower are not the only weapons I have available to deal with my screwups. I accept that there is an unfathomable power greater than myself that can help me, but I do not have to call this power "God."

3. I will willingly rely on whatever I choose to call the God of my understanding.

4. I will honestly and fearlessly take a close look at myself.

5. I will face my mistakes. Without deception or making excuses, I will admit them to myself, the God of my understanding, and another person.

6. I will be truly willing to change. I will recognize that change, even for the good, is not comfortable, but that feeling uncomfortable is no excuse to keep screwing up.

WITH GENERAL SCREWUPS

7. I will take a deep breath and ask to change with all my mind and heart.

8. I will make a list of the people I've harmed and willingly accept that, for my own peace of mind, I need to make amends to each of them.

9. I will make whatever amends I can to those I've injured without doing further damage to anyone.

10. I will fearlessly take a daily look at my thoughts and behavior. When I realize I've goofed up, I will promptly admit it.

11. I will develop the habit of staying in close touch with the God of my understanding.

12. I will commit myself to practice these principles in everything I do.

How to Give Up Constructively

STEP ONE

I WILL ACCEPT THAT MY SCREWUPS ARE HURTING ME AND OTHER PEOPLE, BUT I AM POWERLESS TO STOP DOING THEM.

If you've read this far, you and I have a lot in common. We both know what it's like to be completely mystified by some aspect of our own behavior. It doesn't have to be an addiction. It can be nothing more serious than eating an entire bag of corn chips, watching an episode of *Law and Order* for the fourth time, or losing our tempers when our adolescent child sulks again. The point is we are both intimately familiar with that oh-no-I'm-doing-it-again feeling. It sits like an iron knot inside us. We beat ourselves up a bit over it, time passes, the knot dissipates, we feel better, and we earnestly promise ourselves that next time we'll make a different choice.

Only next time, for some incomprehensible reason, we *don't*. We seem stuck responding in a way we'd rather not. So, we move on to Plan B. We puff ourselves up, read a few more self-help books, go to a therapist, and make a few solemn vows, all in a sincere attempt to master ourselves. We can *lick* this thing, we tell ourselves. We're *tough*. After all, we're still here, aren't we?

And maybe we do lick it, for a while. But then we get blindsided by stress, forget Plan B, and end up with an iron knot inside us that is twice as big as before. We feel overwhelmed by anger at ourselves and perhaps a little frightened. What is going on here? What has happened to our self-control? We begin to flirt with despair. Why, oh why, can't we do just this one thing differently? Maybe therapy has shown us *why* we do it, but we still can't seem to change the behavior itself. The hard truth is that we're really and truly powerless over this particular aspect of ourselves.

What's So Hot about Being Powerless?

The word "powerless" used to make me want to stomp my foot and say, "I am not!" It's one of the tricky Twelve-Step terms I've redefined completely while working this program. In our culture, admitting you are powerless signifies weakness, impotence, and ineffectiveness. In a Twelve-Step sense, admitting you are powerless simply means you've developed the strength to be completely honest with yourself.

I was horrified when I first realized what Step One meant. Was it seriously suggesting I was supposed to look at my life as it really was? Good grief! Where was the fun in that? What was wrong with a little honest pretending if it got me through the day with my head held high? It took me a long time to realize that what I'd made up and called my life wasn't really much fun. It has taken me years to peel back the layers of elaborate explanations I used to excuse my screwy behavior.

First, I had to recognize the fact that I'd been a spin doctor for years. And why not? I had an image to maintain—culturally, intellectually, and emotionally—even if it sometimes conflicted with reality. Although I didn't lie to the rest of the world very much, I lied to myself a *lot*. I also had the deeprooted habit of unconsciously blaming circumstances or other people for my own actions. Consequently, when I ran into Step One, being honest with myself was about as foreign to me as exploring the Arctic.

Looking back, all my trials and errors seem pointless and a bit sad. The Twelve Steps allowed me to recognize my past mistakes and screwups for what they were, learn from them, and leave them behind. I remember my failures, but I don't obsess about them. My Buddhist friends kindly describe my situation back then by saying I did the best I could with the tools and knowledge I had available. Today I have different tools and knowledge, and all I want is keep my eyes and heart open, my brain alert, and my sense of humor accessible. Then I want to look my day right in the eye and get on with it.

Right now I suggest you simply recognize any behavior you currently have that you wish you didn't. *Just look at it.* Don't pass judgment on yourself or roll around in guilt or anxiety.

Don't review your well-researched justifications or crank up your defiance. Just sit calmly and think, "I do this and I'd really like to cut it out."

Then say it out loud. Hear yourself honestly admit your screwup.

You've just begun to change.

How I Got to Step One

I'm a card-carrying baby boomer, a mature rock 'n' roller, part of the generation of women who came of age in the late '60s and early '70s with the aim of getting as far away from Mamie Eisenhower's bangs and Donna Reed's apron as we could. I wanted to live life, not plan it. I believed in achievable peace, and that love and friendship make the world go 'round. I had little interest in security, propriety, or how much money I could stash in the bank. I reached sexual maturity post-pill and pre-AIDS, so I had a lot of freewheeling good times, as you can imagine.

Then gradually, over the years, the fun began to turn sour. I now firmly believe that various devils—with small *d's*, please—are after each and every one of us, tantalizing us with opportunities to screw up. Experimentation can be good—we experiment, we learn, and we move on. Screwing up is bad. Screwing up often begins as experimentation, but then latches onto us and turns into behavior we're not comfortable with.

When I was a teenager, I was not experienced enough to separate screwups from healthy rebellion, and so I think those devils began winning over parts of me about the same time I began wearing braces. I have actual evidence to support this in the poem I added to a ninth grade English paper:

Temptation lurks in front of her.
Unseen she can take
To satisfy her craving self
A piece of chocolate cake.
A battle fought, a battle lost;
But somehow there's no sorrow.
The diet that's been long put off
Can always start tomorrow.

I don't remember anything about the paper, except being all puffed-up by the A++ I got on it. But I do remember that silly poem. It has knocked about in my head for decades along with cheerleading routines, names of best friends and favorite teachers, the oddity of looking down to see breasts growing out my front, and how disturbingly good it felt to dance close to a boy.

I have a notebook of poems from those years. All are dreadfully serious except for the one about chocolate cake. When I wrote it, I was already zooming up toward 5'8" and was as thin as a wafer. I could have eaten all the chocolate cake I wanted, and yet, for some reason, I wrote a ditty about how I should not eat any. Our weight obsessed culture must have already started to sink its claws into me, because even though I was young and skinny, I still felt guilty about eating anything fattening. I had already begun to feel at odds with myself, out of control, and distrustful of my own impulses. I'd already started the deadly cycle of telling myself I shouldn't do something, doing it anyway, and then feeling bad for doing it. Those flirtatious little devils had begun burrowing into my psyche and making themselves right at home. My sense of self was already becoming buried in my screwups.

Inner Peace, Where Are You?

It's difficult for us, even as adults, to separate experimentation from dancing with those pesky little devils. Of course, we can always turn our backs on temptation. I now live surrounded by people who do just that. The Shenandoah Valley of Virginia is home to many Old Order Mennonites, people who deliberately set their lives apart and simply turn their backs on many of the things the rest of us feel we can't do without. They do this in order to keep their focus firmly on God, instead of on what they see as a bunch of less fulfilling diversions.

I pass these fascinating people all the time on the road, driving their buggies or riding their bicycles. I shop beside them at the grocery store. And I am always agog at how peaceful and happy most of them look. But the simple fact is I am *not* an Old Order Mennonite. I want to live my life, not reinvent it, and my life means being a journalist, a wife, a mother, and a keeper of three cats. It means multitasking to the max. It means that I need a car, I don't have time to can tomatoes, and I couldn't step out in a long dress and bonnet. Nevertheless, I yearn for the inner peace that emanates from the Old Order Mennonites.

What Does Inner Peace Feel Like?

I think it's important for you, right now at the beginning of the Steps, to be able to imagine what inner peace feels like. Do you have a memory that brings you back to what it felt like to be a child with the day stretched before you like a great, golden gift? It can be a memory of a place you liked to go, or a person you liked to be with. It can be a memory of anything that triggers feelings of both fundamental security and infinite possibility. Remember, we're talking about a child's version of infinite possibilities—the anticipation of the delights ahead from having a whole day to live exactly where you are right now.

For me that memory is my grandparents' house in Vermont. When I was a little girl, we used to spend three blessed weeks there every summer. It was a sprawling New England complex composed of a house, sheds, a carriage house, and barns, all full of places for a child to lounge and hide. At night, we grandchildren were stashed on cots on a second-floor porch, and we fell asleep to the sound of murmured grown-up conversation from the porch below. I don't remember ever hearing an angry voice in that house. Nor do I remember anything that was remotely passive-aggressive or manipulative. Life there felt simple, straightforward, and happy. In the barns, I could climb a ladder, reach the hayloft, and read away a rainy afternoon. There were rambling attics waiting for exploration, filled with a century's worth of family possessions that were no longer useful, but were too good to throw away.

And there was my grandmother. She was a spectacularly unspectacular woman who calmed everything she touched. Everyone behaved themselves better around her, and everyone relaxed. All the twisted complications of my rather tense home life disappeared for those three weeks in Vermont. I could stop trying so hard and just live. Life was not problem-free, but the problems never ruled. My grandmother ruled. To me that is what inner peace feels like.

I have always carried the memory of how I felt at my grandparent's house inside me as an emotional talisman. Even in my most turbulent years, I would dream about living in that house again. I have never *not* hungered to have that feeling back, and believe me, I have tried all kinds of screwy ways to get it back. In my twenties and thirties, I imagined that the right man could give it to me, so I should keep searching and marrying until I found him. But even back then, long before I began working the Steps, there were always moments when my rock 'n' roll world stopped, and I could see how far I was veering away from any path that would lead me where I wanted to go. One incident in particular haunts me, for it was one of the few times another person saw through my act completely.

Johnny

A couple of careers ago, I co-owned a couple of restaurants in Charlottesville, Virginia. A sweet, young man named Johnny was my dishwasher for many of those years. Johnny was schizophrenic and so was unable to make stable connections with people. Schizophrenics are not supposed to be able to empathize, but they sometimes have the ability to see others with a clarity that stops the heart.

Just before I left the restaurant business, the staff threw a birthday party for me. At that time I thought of myself as a thirty-something Bebop Queen. I came to the party with my latest man, and, much to my surprise and delight, Johnny was there. He came lunging through the crowd and thrust a dog-eared envelope at me. Inside were eleven dollars, a five and six ones. "Why Johnny," I said, "What's this for?"

He looked directly at me, which was hard for him, and said, "That's so you'll always have money to get home."

My heart stopped when he said that. I remember thinking,

"The truth is I am lost. Johnny knows it and is trying his best to help me."

It was probably the only real conversation I had at that party. For one minute in that frantic night, I was able to see that I was in deep trouble. I was nobody's Bebop Queen. I was a lonely and frightened woman who didn't know what the hell she was doing, and so she hid out in crowds.

Right then, someone came over and the dancing started. I pushed that moment with Johnny deep down inside me, buried it under the noise, spin-doctoring and small lies that kept my mind occupied in those days. But I never forgot it, and I will always hold Johnny close in my heart because he cared enough to tell me the truth.

Bouncing Off the Bottom

Substance abuse is my flagship screwup, the one that led me to the Twelve Steps. I suppose my dangerous using started in my late thirties. I had begun to wear out from the effort of spinning myself for myself. I felt unhappy, confused, and scared, and I was unwilling to own any of these emotions. So I began drinking and taking anything that would dull my feelings. Of course, I only felt worse for using downers and alcohol—when I could still feel.

Adult emotional pain is so complicated. It defies easy understanding and grinds you down. When I began slipping into substance abuse, I'd gotten to the point where I just wanted the pain to stop for a while. I wanted to rest. I wanted my head to be quiet. If I couldn't go back to being a child at my grandparents' home, at the very least I wanted to go somewhere else for a few hours.

Was I a substance abuser because I was in emotional pain, or was I in emotional pain because I was a substance abuser? I didn't know then, and I still don't know now. At first, I fed my habit mostly in secret. Very few people even suspected I might have a problem. I'd act out destructively perhaps once a month. Bad feelings would boil inside me. I'd suppress them as long as I could, then feed them with alcohol or pills and ride this unstable mindset toward a crash as though it were a long, dangerous wave.

My substance abuse bottom came fairly quickly once I started slow dancing with alcohol and pills. My binging began to go public, and when I drank I turned impossible. One night, high on wine and low on life, I decided to walk down to a friend's house. The friend was not inclined to invite me in. I don't blame him in the least, since it would have done neither of us any good for him to listen to my crazed ravings. In desperation, he finally called the sheriff. Some nice deputies came and took me home, but I was too far gone on old grief and new booze to stay put. I walked back to my friend's house. Once again he called the cops, and, once again, they came and took me home.

My own behavior that night is impossible for me to romanticize or justify. I distinctly remember what my feelings were on that mid-winter eve, and they were the same feelings I've heard described by almost everyone I've known who's suffered from substance abuse. My feelings were neither romantic nor unique. They were the common, garden-variety, overblown feelings of self-pity produced by the self-medication of substance abusers. My heart and soul hurt like hell, I'd fueled my pain with alcohol, and then acted out badly. In those days, I thought alcohol was the road to truth, but of course, alcohol was the road to nowhere. That night "nowhere" became an increasingly scary place to be alone, and I felt increasingly desperate.

Back I went to my friend's house for the third time.

Different cops came this time, and they were far less patient. It seemed at the time like some dreadfully indecent cosmic joke, but these big guys with guns arrested me, felt me up, and then locked me up for a night in the county jail. For that one night, my life was reduced to a cage of concrete and bars.

It has taken me years to be able to talk openly about that night. I'm charming and cultivated. I'm a groovy, fearless risk taker. People admire me, and say I'm wonderful! How could I have been responsible for getting myself locked up in a crummy county jail? It has taken me a long time to get my head straight enough to realize that my night in jail is as much a part of the real me as my early acceptance to college, and that I couldn't edit episodes out of my own life and expect to live at peace with myself.

One Giant Step for Martha

That night in jail was my Step One night—the night I first admitted complete powerlessness. As I sat on the narrow, concrete sleeping shelf and waited out the long darkness, I quietly realized I had tried every way I knew to make my life work, and that this cage was where I'd landed myself. I had nothing else left to try on my own. I behaved the way I behaved, and by myself I was powerless to change. I was out of explanations and excuses. I looked into the future and didn't like what I saw. I looked at myself and finally saw the unvarnished truth: I didn't have a clue how to get off a train that was racing toward oblivion.

All the people I've met who are involved in substance abuse recovery have such remembered moments of clarity. They stand out in our pasts like blobs of red paint on a white wall. We use them to remember what happens when we don't accept our powerlessness over either the substance we've abused or any number of other things in life, both great and small.

I'm still a mess in a lot of small ways, but I'm a cheerful mess these days. As a good Twelve Stepper, I claim progress, not perfection. I don't flirt with self-destruction anymore in any form. I recognize those seductive little devils for exactly what they are, little devils. What I want to emphasize now is that the start of recovery for me—the beginning of what felt like the long, slow turn of a battleship—was the *acceptance of my messiness.* This meant admitting that inside I was about as serene as an ant colony that's been poked by a sharp stick, and I had no idea what to do about it.

That's all there was to my Step One. I recognized there were things in my life that weren't working (substance abuse, for starters), that I'd tried to fix them and failed, and that I was giving up control of the effort.

I'm sure you can relate to feeling powerless to control some part of yourself, or you wouldn't be reading this. I've never met anyone who isn't bothered in some way by how they think or behave. Over the years, I've watched friends battle all kinds of dysfunction in their lives with their weapons of choice—will power, therapy, self-help, support groups, denial, prescription drugs, illegal drugs, moving around, changing jobs, changing partners, changing hair color, buying themselves things, or developing new hobbies—all of which delivered only partial or temporary change.

The longer I work the Twelve Steps and look around me, the more strongly I feel that letting go of *any* behavior that robs us of inner peace, whether it's life-threatening or just an annoying ankle-biter, begins with our ability to be honest. I've never seen anything other than Step One honesty initiate a transformative process that really worked.

Right here at Step One is where working the Twelve Steps begin to veer away from the accepted self-help norm. Self-help tells us new ways to get cracking and get that part of ourselves under our own control again. Step One, however, asks us to do the exact opposite. Step One asks us not only to recognize, but also *to be comfortable with* our complete powerlessness over those same bothersome parts of ourselves. At first, that may seem like a lunatic's paradox. However, years of experience have taught me that any behavior I am uncomfortable with is nurtured by my own unwillingness to accept the fact that I am powerless over it.

Try a Little Powerlessness

When you're ready, sit quietly and say, "This is what I do that I don't like, and I can't quit doing it on my own." Mean it. Then stop. Period. End of Step. There is nothing else to it. I don't know how you will experience such a straightforward admission of powerlessness, but it took great self-discipline for me to keep it that simple. I'd gotten used to working much, much harder at everything during the years I'd thought it was all up to me.

THE KICK START

- Ask yourself, "What do I do that I'd rather not do?" Write them all down. Yes, you need to make a list! Keep it simple and tell the truth. Skip the amateur psychology about why you do each one, but don't leave anything out that causes you discomfort. No one is going to see this but you.

- Pick the behavior that makes you the most uncomfortable; the one that does the most damage to your health, your relationships, and your life. Think objectively about the one behavior you've picked. Does it really make you uncomfortable, or do you just feel that it *should* make you uncomfortable? In other words, if you eat chocolate in moderation, why do you think you should stop completely? Is it your doctor's advice, or do you think you should stop because it tastes so good that it makes you feel guilty? If the latter is true, maybe the behavior you should tackle first is feeling guilty just to torture yourself.

- List what you've done to try to stop doing whatever it is that makes you so uncomfortable; books you've read, groups you've joined, medication you've tried, and therapies you've undertaken.

- Write down the results of each attempt you've listed to stop the behavior. *Don't judge yourself at all.* Stick to the facts please, just the facts. Pretend you are dispassionately reporting on someone else's attempts to control a behavior.

- Put in writing what you had planned to do next to stop this particular behavior. Then look honestly at the likelihood of your success. Are you optimistic that this action will help you control whatever it is you do that makes you uncomfortable? If yes, then you should try it, because you still believe there is something you can do on your own. If no, are you willing to accept living the rest of your life acting in a way that makes you uncomfortable? In other words, can you give up your discomfort and live with a flaw you can't change?

- If you believe you can, go for it. See if you really can live comfortably with the consequences of that behavior.

- If you find you can't live with the consequences, then admit that you are helpless when it comes to this one behavior. That's it for now. Stop right there. You don't have to wallow in guilt and frustration, but you do have to accept in every fiber of your being that you are helpless. Don't worry about what to do next. There are eleven more steps to go!

2

Baby Step toward Alice

STEP TWO

I WILL RECOGNIZE THAT MY BRAIN AND WILLPOWER ARE NOT THE ONLY WEAPONS I HAVE AVAILABLE TO DEAL WITH MY SCREWUPS. I ACCEPT THAT THERE IS AN UNFATHOMABLE POWER GREATER THAN MYSELF THAT CAN HELP ME, BUT I DO NOT HAVE TO CALL THIS POWER "GOD."

I've never been conventionally religious, but Step Two led me to a strong, nontraditional faith in the God of my understanding. I didn't have to attend church or sign on to any particular dogma to work Step Two. All I needed to do was summon enough rigorous honesty and daring to be truly open-minded and open-hearted. The same goes for you. Faith in God, according to the Steps, does not require any specific religious beliefs.

If you are already a believer, I'm not questioning your beliefs in the least. I do, however, trust that you won't hide behind them or use them as easy answers to complicated questions. In other words, no matter what your current state of belief or non-belief is, I challenge you not to be afraid to change.

Is that enough of a spiritual dare to keep you reading? I hope so. Now here's the story of my own Step Two, told in the hope that it will help you through your own.

Meeting God as Alice

When I first came nose to nose with the Steps, any notion of faith was as hard for me to swallow as a green persimmon. Ever eaten a persimmon before it's been sweetened by frost? It is the Dementor of the mouth. It sucks all the moisture out of your tongue and leaves you unable to find joy even in the taste of pizza.

For years, that was how I experienced almost all public talk about faith. I was raised an agnostic in the heart of the Bible Belt. God, as fervently portrayed by fundamentalists, roamed the classrooms of my elementary school like an angry hall monitor. One year my teacher led the entire class in Monday prayers for me because I didn't go to Sunday school. I asked my father if I could lie and say I *had* gone. Pop calmly replied that I could not.

As a result, I grew up with the suspicion that God was a punitive, nay-saying deity more interested in control than in saving souls. Being surrounded by obstreperous religiosity you can't buy into is almost as lonely as a bad marriage. However, looking for God, or some form of saving, orderly grace (including scientific skepticism), is one of humanity's persistent quests.

I was, however, never so annoyed by the noise of Bible thumping while growing up, that I couldn't see the comfort and guidance religion brought to many people. I've experienced waves of spiritual hunger all my life. I was a Quaker for a while. I flirted with Presbyterianism, Buddhism, Unitarianism, and general do-goodism. Nothing fit. Nothing brought me dependable comfort, guidance, enlightenment, or inner peace.

Emmylou Harris' fearless outlook on change accidentally gave me my spiritual road map. Take her hair, for example. Trace it through album covers, and you'll notice it mutates from long and dark, to short and dark, to streaked with gray, to losing those streaks, then back to long and unabashedly, completely gray. Ms. Harris' music is just like her hair. You can hear her remarkable evolution from album to album, all held together by underpinnings of exacting musicianship. She has always been brave enough to discard what made sense last year for what she knows to be true *right now.* I want to be like that, brave enough to change in the face of new knowledge and the passing of time—and that includes changing my conception of faith.

Admitting I had faith in God was my version of coming out of the closet. On the surface, it felt like a betrayal of my family's firm faith in the life of the mind. The way some people talk about God still makes me cringe, because they use such drippy, limiting clichés that are laden with social and political implications. It has always seemed to me that Yahweh, the great I Am, is the one unfathomable mystery of the universe. I think the whole point is to relate to Yahweh by wordless faith, not wordy show.

I solved my personal discomfort with religious language by thinking of the great I Am as Alice. It's perfectly okay to talk naturally to anyone named Alice. An Alice isn't preoccupied with worship and loyalty oaths. She's pleased by loyal companionship and real effort. And an Alice is not fooled by show. Instead, she simply expects me to behave myself.

The Long and Winding Road to Alice

If you're like me, your first spiritual experience arrived before you even knew what it was. When I was about eight, I had an honest-to-Alice, out-of-body experience. It happened because the food on other people's plates has always been more attractive to me than food on my plate. Growing up, I would secretly scavenge in the kitchen after I'd cleared the table. One evening when I was furtively picking through left-over fried chicken, I choked. What followed was a pretty classic near-death experience. My short life passed before me. I rose out of my skinny, four-foot body and began whooshing through a tunnel toward a welcoming light. I knew instinctively there was nothing to be afraid of, that I was going somewhere safe. My mother must have heard me trying to breathe because she came into the kitchen, whacked me on the back, dislodged the chicken, and sent me whooshing back into my body. Then she gave me a stiff talking-to about the risks of scavenging, and that was that. I didn't think then about whether the light I was headed toward was God, but neither did I forget the episode.

I did have some religious training at an all-girls boarding school in New England. While I was there I was exposed to an intelligent brand of high Episcopalian Christianity. The school's religiosity was thoroughly structured, but pitched at a much lower key than the strident, simplistic kind I'd grown up with. Church was required on Sundays, but as a safe gesture of sweet rebellion, I went in white gloves, a hat, a coat, and my pajamas.

I was required to take a Bible study class. Our cheerful, tolerant school chaplain was willing to take my insistent, querulous disbelief seriously and talk to me without preaching. I wanted a God that made sense to me personally. I wanted a logical system, without meanness, that would add up to a God I could conceptualize. Finally, the chaplain managed to get through to me that God was what God was, that my conceptualizing was my conceptualizing, and that the two were quite separate. He introduced me to the concept that faith is the only way humans can transcend their own intellectual limitations and become open to God's power and love. I didn't buy it. I didn't develop faith, but I did file this new understanding away for possible future use.

Groping My Way toward the Light

I think I began going to Quaker meeting in my turbulent late thirties mainly for a chance to sit quietly in the building. It was the beginning of my seriously, self-destructive years. My daughter was gone, I'd ended my second marriage, and I was going through relationships like high-stakes poker hands, riding high and bluffing a lot. My heart was not sad as much as seriously frayed. Most of my sketchy income came from freelancing in broadcast journalism. I had no financial or emotional security at all.

The Quaker meeting house just north of Winchester,

Virginia, felt as peaceful as I was not. The building is late eighteenth century, perfectly plain with big windows that look out on the sky and surrounding green fields. It was a silent meeting, and I liked to sit and watch the faces of families who had been Quakers for generations. Those faces were so serene, so *present* there in the meeting, upturned to the light from all those windows. And there I was, hardly able to sit still. How, oh how, did they get those faces? I'd watch them and feel drawn to something unnamable that was always just out of my reach, like the ever-retreating horizon.

Those Quakers were the first breed of religious folks I'd met who kept their expressions of faith simple. I remember a woman telling me that the time she spent in church was like dessert or a short vacation. It was a treat for her just to sit there and commune with the Light—the presence of God—without any interference from the rest of the noisy world. She said her true faith was practiced in living day-to-day among the small temptations, petty annoyances, minor disappointments, and fatigue of all the other hours of the week. This was when peace and love were not one-syllable words, but complicated inter-personal situations with no clear right or wrong solutions. This was when she found out if she was really able to live in the Light; this was when being a Quaker was a challenge.

I stopped attending Quaker meeting when I changed towns, but I filed the image of those light-filled faces away, as well. It was at about that time I began to visualize choice as a circular continuum. All my options stood side by side, sur-rounding me like a circle of small children eager to be chosen for kickball, grinning, jumping up and down, waving their arms and screaming, "Take me! Take me!" It was always perfectly obvious that light shone clearly over one or two choices, and varying shades of darkness hovered over the others. I was never so dumb or numb that I didn't realize I felt a greater sense of *internal* orderliness if I chose to act in a way that was in the light, no matter how disorderly the *external* consequences might be.

Choice, however, was still a frenetic activity for me in those days. There were so many competing voices shouting caveats and disclaimers. They claimed fatigue, frustration, job stress, relationship stress, and any other kind of stress as perfectly good reasons to choose something other than that which would bring me peace of mind. In those days, I think I *was* my stress. Stress was my badge of accomplishment, my proof that I was in the game. If I let it go, how would I know I was really part of anything meaningful?

My First Prayer

I said my first real prayer for help while dealing with my second ex-husband. He is a very nice man, but he hovered over my life during those messy years after our divorce like an angry toad. Our conversations, unlike those with my first ex-husband, *never* went well. So one day there I was, helpless again, trying to remain rational and in control of myself while this man skillfully hit every button in my psyche. My first prayer born of helplessness was a real skeptic's prayer, "Lord, I'm making a mess of this again and I can't stop. If you're there, could I have a little help behaving myself, right here, right now?"

Well, who'd a thunk it! For the first time in my life, I did not respond to that man's button pushing! I came out of that particular conversation without feeling I'd made a sad situation worse. Of course, I was humiliated that my second ex-husband had reduced me to praying. Prayer had always seemed silly and vaguely debasing for a sentient being such as myself, rather like a grown-up's letter to Santa Claus. I buried the fact that I had prayed deep in my mind like a particularly embarrassing secret. But the fact was that I had prayed and, as a result, had been able to behave.

It wasn't lost on me that I hadn't prayed to change him back to the nice guy he'd been when we were together. Instead, I'd prayed to be able to cope with him as he was now. What a concept!

Crawling from Screwups to Alice

Bob Marley sings about our having many rivers to cross in life, and I still had a big one left to swim. It was filled with alcohol and pills, which made me feel astoundingly terrible and finally landed me in jail. But even I can recognize the truth when I'm clubbed on the head with it by getting locked up, and the truth was that when I fueled my body with drugs and alcohol, my life jumped in the toilet. Ergo, I had to stop using completely.

I immediately began working *at* the Steps, but I left all the God stuff out of them. I was, after all, doing this stepping stuff because I wanted to stay out of jail, not because I wanted to find divine truth.

Although I had stopped using, I was still quite the little snobbette. The slammer, however, had left a therapeutic stink on me that has never quite washed off. Unless you're there on principle, there's nothing esteem-building about being caged up. My night in jail had made me much more honest. As the weeks and months went by and I slogged my way deeper into the Steps, I was surprised to find myself cleansed of most of the limitations of my faux superiority. I began to see the simple truth: I am a person among other people, nothing more, nothing less. Once I stopped spinning myself to myself, I was able to take what I'd learned in books, in therapy, from two failed marriages, from doing a bad job of raising a great child, and *use* it. I was finally able to look at myself and the world with clear eyes.

After that came the leap. I had no blinding epiphany. To borrow a phrase from Yeats, I slouched toward faith. My embracing of Alice was an awkward business, full of false starts. It began in earnest when I noticed that some of the people who were also working the Steps had faces reminiscent of those peaceful, light-filled Quakers' faces. I began to listen to their spiritual experiences without a running edit on their word choice. I stopped using semantics to make the leap of faith wider and realized that what I called God, what I said to God, and how I thought about God only mattered to me. It certainly didn't matter to her. What mattered to her was that I use her power for healing, for good, and for love.

The Past, as Seen from the Present

A couple of years before I began working the Twelve Steps, I moved back to Charlottesville. On the outside, I was the same carefree rock 'n' roller I'd always been. Inside, however, I was beginning to seriously wear down. I couldn't tolerate a regular job, so I put together a pastiche of freelance activities that paid the rent. One of them was writing a regular column for *Albemarle Magazine.* Here is part of one I wrote a couple of years before I got sober. I thought at the time it was about a child's Christmas in Greensboro, North Carolina, but I now see it was about my submerged yearning for faith.

> I'm not going to sit here, single and in my forties, and pretend that November and December are the safe, magic months that they were when I was a child. . . . As I've grown older, I believe more and more firmly in the devil. It yaps at my heels and tempts me to indulge in fear—the great limiting, dark side of experience. Christmas is still the best defense I know against the devil. Christmas always bids me to find the Light and face it.
>
> There's a line in "God Rest Ye Merry, Gentlemen" that talks about the "holy tide of Christmas." Now growing up, I had my Beach Boy records stacked right alongside old Dylan Thomas. When I sing that line, I always have a vision and this is what I see.
>
> We are all out there together, on the vast Ocean of Life, sitting on our surfboards and scared out of our minds—which is the general human state of mind. Then, someone yells, "Surf's up!" We turn toward the horizon and here it comes, the holy tide of Christmas.
>
> Suddenly, we're all up on our boards, catching that giant wave and riding it, full of joy, all the way to the beach.

Revisiting Your Own Spiritual History

Sometime in my thirties, I read C. S. Lewis' *Mere Christianity.* In this short, infinitely entertaining book, Lewis traces his own experience of being born again—although his was an intellectual's decorous Christian conversion that

landed him in the Church of England. The book is closely reasoned and very funny. C. S. Lewis reminded me of my prep
school chaplain, willing to take arguments and doubts seriously, not just shout them down. Lewis says such comforting
things as, "Besides being complicated, reality, in my experience, is usually odd." And, "There has been a great deal of soft
soap talked about God for the last hundred years. That is not
what I am offering. You can cut all that out."

Looking at his work from the broadest of angles, C. S.
Lewis maintains that we humans have a natural hunger for
God. If C. S. Lewis is right, as I firmly believe he is, you'll find
that you, too, have a secret yen to believe in some power
greater than yourself. It sits there inside you as a kind of spiritual itch you can't seem to scratch.

What I suggest you do is take some time over the next week
or month or year—there's no time limit on this—and wander
back through your own spiritual past. Revisit your own
moments of hunger, clarity, and revelation—any experience
that tempted you to peek beyond a world you can quantify,
measure, explain, or deconstruct, refer to science, or a cultural
relativist. Even if you responded to them with intellectual eye-
rolling, bring those moments out and revisit them.

Perhaps the heart of the problem in owning this yen is the
same for you as it was for me: conceptualizing the form that
power should take. Before I bumped into Alice, God was a
mystery that lots of other people seemed to understand perfectly and were eager to help me understand as well. The problem for me was that the gods most of these people pushed at
me during my non-believing years seemed limited, not limit-
less. Any help these gods had to offer seemed contingent on

my swearing some sort of allegiance—rather like the one a feudal lord demanded from his vassals. Was God really such a control freak? If so, then God was not for me. That's not the kind of relationship I want with another person, let alone with the great I Am.

Perhaps that conceptual confusion is at the heart of the God quandary for you. Or perhaps it is something else? All I'm encouraging you to do right now is explore your head, your heart, and your history. If that spiritual itch is in you, acknowledge it. Acknowledge your hunger for *something* meaningful and powerful outside yourself.

Making the Leap

When I was a kid, I had a friend who had a two-story hay barn with a world-class rope swing. I would catch the rope with a hook, stand at the edge of the loft, straddle a giant knot, and leap into space. For an instant I'd fall, then the rope would catch, and I'd fly out over the vast floor below, soaring up toward the sky spread out before me through the big, open, second-floor doors. For a couple of seconds, I was nothing but happy, did nothing but live.

That's the closest I can come to describing what became available to me once I finally made the leap of faith. Once I said hello to Alice, I dumped a whole lot of useless angst and pointless complications, and simply got on with living. It was again possible to feel happy—not ecstatic, not triumphant, not thrilled—just happy.

Your own leap of faith will be like a lot like the birth behind you and the death ahead of you. It's a natural part of life that you must do alone. But unlike birth and death, you do have a choice about this one. To leap, or not to leap, that is the question.

All I can offer you as encouragement to make such a leap yourself is the story of my own experiences with Alice. All I ask is that you don't argue with me about them. They aren't dogma, they aren't myths, and they aren't speculation. I ask you to accept my experiences for what they are, something that really happened in another person's life.

Alice and I are tight these days. There's a connection inside me to her that is always available. It doesn't shout, it doesn't clamor for attention, and it doesn't struggle for control. It is, indeed, "a still small voice" that is always there, and it is what connects me in a meaningful way to the rest of the world.

How it does this, I don't know and I don't care. Whatever I have to say about metaphysical structures and systems is all hogwash—pleasant, intellectually challenging hogwash or emotionally satisfying hogwash, but hogwash nonetheless. What I do know is that, if I sit quietly and ask Alice to stay in the driver's seat, then I am able to behave and feel better than I ever could if I were driving myself. By better, I don't mean anything sexy or complicated. I mean kinder, gentler, and less judgmental. I'm able to listen. I'm able to keep my temper. I'm able to tolerate and sometimes even love other people.

Fake It 'til You Make It

I've found over the years that with Alice's help, I gradually became able to *behave* like a person who felt the way I wanted to feel. As I behaved better, I had fewer complications and anxieties to deal with, and I actually began to *feel* better.

Slowly, I gained confidence in Alice as a rock-solid source of strength that will always give me the ability to behave.

So, if and when you are comfortable, acknowledge your hunger for a power greater than yourself and say hello to Alice, George, the Source, God or Whatever. Don't worry about what he, she, or it looks like, or where he, she, or it lives. Just reach out and, metaphorically speaking, shake hands. Then simply live with the relationship for a while and see how it feels.

That's all there is to Step Two.

THE KICK START

Again, write everything down, and spend some time on each point.

- What do you believe about God right now?

- Are you willing to open up and take help from any- one or anything, or do you still believe that you're on your own dealing with your hurt, confusion, and shame?

- If you're an agnostic or an atheist . . .

   o What experiences have you had in nature or with other people that felt scientifically unquantifiable? In other words, what spiritual experiences have you had? Make a list, and don't worry if this feels dopey at first. This is just you coming clean to yourself about your inner life.

   o Look carefully at what you've written. Have you shied away from acknowledging the impact of those experiences on you? Why? What exactly holds you back from acknowledging some kind of spiritual connection in your life? Your head? Your heart? Your pride? Your upbringing?

   o You've admitted helplessness over some part of your behavior in Step One. You've made a list of everything else you've tried. You're not ready to accept that you are doomed to live the rest of your life with that behavior. So where else were you planning to turn for help? Are you capable of asking for, and accepting, help in dealing with this situation? Or are you too stubborn, scared, or proud to trust in anything other than yourself?

○ Now, beat down your pride and tell your ego to put a sock in it. Are you rock-solid certain that you have life all figured out? Are you willing to listen with an open mind to folks you respect, who do have faith, when they tell the story of their own leap to belief?

● If you're already a religious person . . .

○ Do you take time daily to commune quietly with the God of your understanding? Do you keep that connection going throughout the day, actively seeking God's warmth and support?

○ In your daily life, do you try to practice what God asks you to do through your conscience, even when it may be inconvenient, unpopular, uncomfortable, or costly?

○ Are you willing to ask God to open you to a more complete relationship between the two of you?

3

We Get by with a Little Help

STEP THREE

I WILL WILLINGLY RELY ON WHATEVER I CHOOSE TO CALL THE GOD OF MY UNDERSTANDING.

Some time ago I sent a friend an encouragement card that I still think about. It showed a Thurberesque drawing of a goat halfway up a flight of stairs, butting heads with a truly formidable riser. The caption inside read, "Fact-to-face with the next step."

It could also have been a drawing of Martha facing Step Three. For me, this step seemed high and hard to climb—probably because it is. This is the point in the Steps where we actually have to begin to walk the walk of faith in our daily lives.

Some Comforting Semantics

Before we go any further, please notice two words in Step Three. The first is "willingly." This means there will be no bribes, entreaties, or pokes with a sharp stick to get you going on this Step or any other. The Twelve Steps are not a recruiting tool designed to get you to sign on to anything. "Willingly" means that you are open to changing your thoughts, your habits, and your spiritual beliefs. Willingness is the best antidote I know to the addictive trait of rigidity, which I always find so terribly limiting in myself or anyone else.

The second word in Step Three to pay particular attention to is "rely." We are to *rely* on this Power, not *depend* upon it. My partnership with God in no way reduces my autonomy, freedom, or responsibility. Instead, Step Three invites me to form an alliance with my God, in which I am simply paying attention to the input of a respected, reliable, and infinitely wise partner in life. I don't worship Alice, but I do count on her. Moreover, I enjoy her company and want to stay as close to her as possible throughout the day.

The only thing I'm really afraid of these days (thank-you, Mr. Roosevelt) is fear, itself. Fear locks me into apathy, dulls my curiosity, and makes me loath to risk change, even for the better. It also operates like acid on my conscience, and these days I want my conscience to be as vigorous as possible. Its soft-spoken, inner voice is my most direct link to Alice, and thus my best defense against self-deception and the strong siren call of the human herd which constantly tries to lure me off in other, less satisfying directions.

A Word about Justification

The Twelve Steps, even though they begin with an admission of helplessness, are not a program of self-flagellation or self-pity. Instead, they are a festival of honesty. And here we are, like that old greeting-card goat, standing face-to-face with Step Three, poised to take on a new partnership with our God.

I wasn't very enthusiastic about doing Step Three. To tell the truth, it remains a daily challenge for me, because it asks me to trust in the God of my understanding—not just *say* I trust, but actually do it. And trust means that I have to be my undecorated self, screwups and all, in Alice's company. I cannot spin reality to make myself appear more successful or more pitiful to her. If I'm going to have a real relationship with God, I have to tell the truth—first to myself and then to her, him, it.

Think about it. If I lie to you (or even just fudge a little), on some level I make nonsense out of our relationship. So it follows that, if I were to profess a belief in the God of my understanding and then lie to that God, I make nonsense out of both that relationship and my relationship with myself. Lying (and this includes making excuses) about my behavior or thoughts makes slogging through a spiritual program built around honesty completely pointless.

The first time I faced Step Three, I was desperate. This stepping stuff felt like my last chance at having a reasonable life. Not to get too sappy about it, but two roads did indeed diverge before me. The one, much less traveled, headed off into the foreign land of reality. The other, very familiar one, led right back into the toilet of my well-spun life.

I remember feeling pretty mulish and grumpy about the whole Step process at this point. If the naked truth be told, I was flat-out uncomfortable with the idea of being myself in *any* relationship, inner or outer. As I've said before, I'd fudged, prevaricated, and spin-doctored to myself for so long that I had only a hazy idea of who I was. But if I were to proceed, much less succeed, with the Twelve Steps, I had to try relating to Alice (and myself) without decorating reality, rationalizing the truth, whining about other people's behavior, or making excuses.

We live in a culture that is very fond of justification. I know that in my old, pre-Step days, I felt certain that if I came up with an explanation for *why* I'd done something stupid, hurtful, or reprehensible, no one would dare hold me accountable. I would somehow be morally off the hook for the consequences of whatever I'd done. In those days, if I behaved in ways I didn't think I should (regularly losing my temper, for example) I would say to myself, "I don't want to do this, but I'm doing it anyway because, for this or that reason, I can't help it." Then I would feel desperately sorry for myself for being emotionally damaged and deeply furious at whomever I currently blamed for that damage. In those days, I was so busy placing blame, being angry, and feeling sorry for myself that I didn't have time to consider how my bad behavior affected the unfortunate folks who'd come within my firing range. It simply never occurred to me that accepting responsibility for the results of my behavior might be the start of the better life for which I was so desperately hungry.

Knowing why we do what we do is certainly important. I'm not knocking psychotherapy, self-help, or the insight and support of friends. The insight of others has helped me face some extremely painful truths about my personal history. It was with their help that I was able to recognize that, in managing my pain, I had set up the dysfunctional behavior patterns that crippled me. However, even after I understood these behavior patterns, I still couldn't change them. I couldn't *think* my way to healthy behavior. I remained in the thrall of the past and its entrenched behavioral and emotional patterns.

The truth was that by giving myself permission to justify my bad behavior, I was giving myself permission to continue doing all those stupid, hurtful, and reprehensible things to myself and other people. Explanations are therapeutic, but making excuses is dysfunctional. Step Three is the point in the Steps when we give up justifying our stupid behavior—first to ourselves, then to our God, then to everyone else.

Enter Alice

Of course, I couldn't straighten this out on my own. I was powerless, not only against pills and booze, but also against the compulsive spin-doctoring of my daily life story. So at some point, I took a deep breath, grabbed onto Alice, stuck my toes into the waters of reality, and began to live real life again.

I found the experience weird, humbling, and unexpectedly relaxing. When I spent time with Alice, I didn't have to pretend to myself or to her about who I was or what I'd done. It reminded me of my experience decades ago when I quit smoking and suddenly had all the time I'd spent with cigarettes for doing other things. After Step Three, I had all the mental and emotional energy available that I'd formerly used to perpetrate fudgings, prevarications, and self-justifications. I could now redirect this energy into having have some real relationships with other people. As a result, I felt better about myself almost right away.

I often refer to my close relationship with God as a partnership, but it feels more like a great romance. A good partnership enlarges our reach and enhances our assets, while at the same time diminishing our weaknesses and making us stronger. But it remains businesslike. A great romance is a good partnership that makes us happy.

Whatever you want to call it, my liaison with the God of my understanding was a tad slow to bloom—it took four decades. I had to exhaust all other options for achieving peace of mind, before I could accept the possibility that Alice might be able to help me stop feeling and acting like such a screwball.

I think our culture is not set up to encourage a romance with God. If you grew up conventionally religious, you may have been taught to fear God. If you're agnostic, you may have decided to forget about God, or you pay the concept lip service at best. Any intimate connection with the divine is so quiet and calm. It goes against our busy, consumeristic society, where the message is: I buy, therefore I am. And it can't be multi-tasked—you can't answer e-mail and commune with God at the same time.

I still have great difficulty with any form of contemplative practice. I'm not, and will never be, the patron saint of reflection. I get a good buzz out of producing under pressure, but I'm pretty sure that the jittery thrill of a good buzz is not taking me any closer to where I want to be inside. I remind myself constantly that what I want and need most is peace of mind and a sense of wholeness in my life. Spending too much time in any fast lane is a sure way to find myself back on the highway to nowhere.

The first two Steps prepared us to give an alliance with God a chance. In Step One we accepted that our screwups hurt us, and that we are powerless to stop them. In Step Two we recognized that a power greater than ourselves could help us stop screwing up. Step Three is where we hold our noses and jump into this pool of practical, yet mystical, truth. We're tired of drowning in dysfunction and guilt, so we're finally ready to take swimming lessons with the God of our understanding.

What Can You Expect from This Alliance?

I've heard stories of alliances with God that produce an immediate and miraculous end to the compulsive abuse of drugs and alcohol. What I experienced, while much less spectacular, eventually proved to be just as useful, amazing, and miraculous. When I began working the Steps, I already had a pretty good record of blasting through physical discomfort, but psychological discomfort was another matter entirely. Before Step Three, I would gamely give up drugs and alcohol for a while, braving headaches and sleep disruption, but then cave at the first whiff of anxiety and scurry back to my sheltering, self-destructive habits. After Step Three, once I had decided to rely on Alice willingly, I discovered a new ability to tolerate the psychological discomfort involved in the reconfiguration of my daily life without drugs and alcohol. I wasn't miraculously reinvented as a habit-free Martha, but I did become a Martha who had the grit and the humor to get through her days—yes, one day at a time—without alcohol and pills. With Alice riding shotgun in my life, I was able to wait out all the grasping, drug-pushing devilettes who'd been taking up a lot of real estate inside my head. Eventually, they got bored and piped down.

An historical fact with which neither you nor I can argue is that, once I turned the mess over to Alice, I was finally able to stop drinking and drugging. I can't explain it, and I don't know how it happened, but I do have to accept that it did happen. And that miracle will stay in place as long as I maintain my reliance on an honest relationship with Alice; as long as I turn my will and my life over to her care.

Taking on a Working Faith in Alice

For me, the crux of faith lies in not knowing exactly how Alice does her thing. It goes against everything in my heredity and upbringing to trust Alice, whose methods I cannot rationally grasp, to take me toward a new and better life, whose shape I cannot control.

Before I began working the Steps, I had faith only in myself. Maintaining a sense of control over my life was more important to me than anything else—including reality, sanity, health, and other people. These days, I'm more and more able to accept that, while I certainly have choices, *I do not have direct control over the circumstances or the results of the choices I make.*

Say, for example, I'm trying to kick cigarettes. You and I are co-workers and you're a real pain. Even though I'm trying to quit smoking and have asked Alice for help, I still don't have the power to stop you from annoying me at a staff meeting. But with Alice at my side, I *can* find the ability to tolerate my annoyance without having to take a cigarette break to deal with it. I don't know how this happens, I just know that it does. I now accept that I can rely on Alice—ask for, and accept, her help and companionship—to give me the ability to stop screwing up my life, no matter what you do in a staff meeting.

My trust in Alice has sometimes been ungraceful, even grudging. I'm still terribly self-conscious about calling myself a person of faith—not to mention writing a book about being one. I feel a bit silly when I *think* about relying on a power greater than myself, so I don't think about it all that much. These days I just do it because it works so much better than what I used to do on my own. My own best thinking landed me in jail; a working faith in Alice has kept me from going back.

I'm confident that Alice is unperturbed by my intermittent skepticism. She appears to have a nonhuman indifference toward control. The Alice of my understanding consistently bestows love, guidance, and peace of mind. She keeps me living in the Light, where I'm able to do the world and myself some good, and out of the musty darkness of the slammer.

How to Finish Step Three

I had the club of substance abuse beating me over my head when I began working the Steps. If you're not addicted to anything, you'll need to be clear once again about the exact nature of your own club—the screwup that has driven you to your knees. At this point, do Step One again and name it. Start your day by saying it out loud in one or two words. Don't focus on the results of doing it, or how you'd like to be different. If you eat too much, forget about your weight. If you tell a lot of little lies, forget the justifications. Focus on the fact that you lie and it makes you feel awful. Then grit your teeth, connect with the God of your understanding as best you can, and ask for help with your lying. Resist the temptation to deliver instructions on how this help should be delivered. Don't worry about whether you're connecting in the right way. The only relevant point is that you're taking your best shot at relying on God. If your experience is like mine, you'll be heard and helped.

Next, for me, there came a habit of ending my day with an informal chat with Alice about how things had gone, not in the eyes of the world, but according to the tugging of my own heart and conscience. Had I been honest? Had I been kind? Had I listened enough? What had I done well? What had I screwed up? I committed myself to full disclosure with Alice. No one else was listening in, and I found it was a relief to end my days facing the unvarnished truth. For one thing, I slept better.

Gradually, over time, I developed a habit of chatting candidly with Alice throughout the day. These days I keep close to her because I've found it's healthy for me in the same way that eating right, working out, and getting enough sleep are healthy for me. The only part of life I can really touch is the present, and I mean to give myself the best chance of enjoying it in a truly satisfying way. Over time, all my chatting with Alice has given me something peaceful deep inside that is beyond the reach of all the rocking and rolling around me. I can look back and see that this sense of peace has quietly wormed its way into my behavior and gently changed it for the better.

I still commit the occasional, behavioral foo-foo, but I do

fewer and fewer things that I don't want to. The single most important step for me in this change was the one we're tackling now: realizing it's safe to be myself, trusting in a power greater than myself for help when I need it, and then relying fully on that power. Not just *believing* in that power, but *relying* upon her, him, or it.

I used to be a fan of the grand plan and the disciplined assault. However, my comfortable and comforting relationship with good old Alice has been forged quietly, almost haphazardly, by including her in the details of my life. I'm still working on this Step. It certainly began with a new ability to tolerate the discomfort of giving up booze and pills, but it has blossomed into lots of interconnected, small changes. The longer I hang out with Alice, the clearer it becomes to me that my responsibility in our partnership is to be honest, to look after only this day's business, and to let the big picture take care of itself.

I still do not find Step Three's commitment to a living faith easy. In many quiet but exacting ways, my pal Alice is one tough cookie. She requires a discipline of spirit that goes against my well-entrenched, self-indulgent, excuse-making grain. She doesn't care much for such things as creative prevarication, passive-aggressive behavior, self-centeredness, wanton outbursts of temper, playing the martyr, doing good works without joy, carrying grudges or resentments of any kind, bitterness, vindictiveness, or harmful gossip. In fact, she's no fun at all in those departments.

What Alice *does* like is companionship, trust, and quiet connection—which I have found to be the three central elements of my faith. I believe a living faith is a freely bestowed gift, but it is picky about where it will take up residence. It will not live in a heart that wants to know "What's in it for me?" It will not live in the same heart as fear. It does not require enemies to survive. It will flee at the first hint of judgmental self-righteousness as fast as I would flee from a skunk in a bad mood.

I'd also like to emphasize that all I feel is at stake for me in accepting Alice's help and guidance is my own inner peace. I don't believe I'll go to hell if I turn my back on God, and then fudge on my income tax, spread hurtful gossip around the office, or eat too much chocolate. I will simply feel separate from Alice and my best self. That means I will become much less peaceful, much less happy, and I will fall back into all my old, unpleasant behavior patterns.

Like all the Steps, this one takes as long as it takes. It's not something you can work harder at and get done faster. Step Three takes real patience. For me, the paradox came in discovering that, with Alice riding shotgun, I had all the patience I needed.

THE KICK START

- What "shoulds" and "don'ts" did you grow up with that influence your life right now? What voices from your past are you still obeying or rebelling against? Make a list of their directives and ask yourself if they still make sense in your life.

- How is your relationship with yourself? Are you comfortable with your own thoughts and feelings? Can you simply let go and happily wander curiously around in your own mind? If not, why not?

- How is your relationship, in general, with other people? Are you comfortable? Are you interested in what they have to say, or are you just waiting until they stop talking so you can start?

- What drives you through the day? Are you goal-oriented? Do you need to control the results of whatever you are doing to feel that it is worthwhile, or do you have some pleasurable and healthy daily activities that are not directed toward producing specific results? Are you able to do anything simply for pleasure, without keeping your eye on the clock and thinking about what you have to do next?

- What do you feel the need to control? Yourself? Your time? Other people? Make a list. Next to it, write down everything you do to control these things. Do your control mechanisms work? Do they make you feel good or bad about yourself? If you gave up each one, what are you afraid would happen? Is that fear realistic?

● Getting down to one specific behavior that bothers you:

○ What excuses do you make when you behave in the way you don't want to behave?

○ Do you seek support, understanding, and permission to continue whatever behavior you tell yourself you want to stop?

○ Do you *need* to feel conflicted about this behavior? Has feeling conflicted become a part of who you are? If so, spend time imagining going through an ordinary day without engaging in whatever behavior you do that you want to stop. How would you feel? Remember, it does you absolutely no good to lie to yourself about any of this.

● In Step Two, you accepted the existence of a power greater than yourself. Are you now willing to make time for that power's company in your daily life? If so, are you willing to let go of the expectation of any specific results from that connection? Are you willing to give faith a try?

4

Losing the Excuses

STEP FOUR

I WILL HONESTLY AND FEARLESSLY TAKE A CLOSE LOOK AT MYSELF.

With Step Four we begin a more serious and measured look at ourselves that will continue through the rest of the Steps. Looking back, I've seen the brilliance of taking this look in specifically defined stages. Proceeding at such a deliberate pace kept my customary defensiveness, guilt trips, and denial at bay. By the end of a Step-driven self-examination, I not only knew myself thoroughly for the first time in my adult life, but was comfortable with myself, as well.

Taking a Whole-istic Approach

Most young women I see in the weight room of my gym appear to assess their bodies as though they were assembled in pieces. They stand before the mirror in the ladies' locker room and critique their thighs, stomachs, and hips independently, with no fundamental enjoyment of the fact that, when taken together, these parts form a healthy, working body. Lifting weights, for these young women, is mostly about appearance—and not even about their appearance as a whole, but about how those individual pieces look. It appears to me they spend an hour every day trying to control what the rest of the world thinks of their butts.

Now there's nothing wrong with your pieces looking good, but I'd find it a pretty unsatisfying goal for lifting weights once, let alone lifting them for an hour every day. I do know something about how much fun it is for a woman to know she's lookin' good. According to the fashion of my day, I was a babe among babes for a long time. Frankly, I've found being let out of the spotlight by developing a few wrinkles and sags, and sinking into middle-age, more emancipating than regretful. I'm a nonentity on the street again, and I do not miss the attention of strangers at all. It feels as though I've been given extra energy and focus to get on with the real business of living.

Of course, as my friends point out, I might miss my youthful, gaudy plumage more if I weren't living so happily with my husband, Charlie. But I don't really think so. My gut opinion about aging is that if we welcome it—or at least accept it—growing older can be a joyous release from the bondage of our lookist culture. It allows us to give up any obligation to stare at pieces of ourselves. We can learn at last to enjoy and accept ourselves as a whole package.

For me, the liberating process of relaxed self-acceptance was given a major kick in the pants by Step Four. I'd long wanted to thumb my nose at a lot of the cultural pressures with which I was uncomfortable, but I just didn't know how to do it—how to turn off the world's noise. Cultural pressures are everywhere we turn. They are as insistent as advertising can make them with its orchestrated assumption that we may look like human beings, but we function as lemmings who are easily led to live and look the same, buy the same things, and have fun in the same expensive ways.

It makes me want to shout "Hooray!" when I see a young woman working out who's obviously lifting simply to get stronger. Some of them are gorgeous by today's standards, others are not. But they are all miles ahead of where women were when I was their age. Life is something they will live, not something they will decorate. Looking good for them will be a natural byproduct of staying healthy and active. They know and respect their bodies, and so they want to take care of them. Or, they love their sport, and they lift because lifting weights improves their sports performance.

In much the same way, Step Four improves our life performance. It's where we begin to know and respect ourselves as whole people. As a result, we begin taking care of what we've really got going for us instead of what we *wish* we had going for us—or what others tell us we *should* have going for us. This is the Step where we begin to get a grip on the simple truth that what we are *inside* is what really makes us feel comfortable living our own lives.

If you're at all like me, I think you'll find that once your insides are in order, your outsides will assume less importance. I invite you to think of Step Four as the beginning of a grand housecleaning of the heart. This is the Popeye Step. When you're done, you'll be able to stand naked in front of a mirror, look yourself up and down, and say without judgment, "I am what I am." You may not like everything you see, but you can now face it honestly, with curiosity, acceptance, and even appreciation.

Let me emphasize right now that this Step is not about self-abasement, but about functional self-acceptance. I made Step Four way too complicated at the beginning, mostly because I didn't want to think of myself as a regular person with regular strengths and weaknesses. My self-image demanded complexity. For a long time I couldn't bear to be honest with myself about myself, or else I simply didn't know how to do it.

What Didn't Work, and What Did

This is what I tried for Step Four that *didn't* work. I sat down with a piece of paper fully prepared to make a list. I stared at the paper for ten minutes or so with a blank, eager mind. Then I began doodling flowers on the paper, because no words were coming and that's all I know how to draw. I jiggled a foot and made a few faces at the flowers on the paper. Then I gave up in disgust because I simply didn't know how to get started.

In the days when Alice was still more of a concept than a companion, I usually felt like either the queen of the world or a con artist, depending upon how my day had gone. I was used to either being angry and blaming other people for my troubles or feeling hopeless about them. Just as actors may feel they're only as good as their last reviews, I felt only as good as my last interpersonal interaction. That's maybe a bit of an exaggeration, but my assessment of myself did go up and down a lot in those days. The result was I noodled and doodled on my piece of paper and wrote down nothing. My unreal life could not be captured on the page. I'd begun to understand myself historically through therapy, but I didn't yet *know* myself. I could have written down what I'd done and why I'd done it, but not who I was.

I finally got through this Step by changing two things about the process. The first was that I formally included a list of my strengths in the inventory of my character. I even gave them pride of place on the page by writing them down first. It was a real light bulb moment, realizing that I needed to own my good points during this inventory process—that the official me needn't be limited to my shortcomings. And I didn't have to wallow endlessly in my character defects to do this Step, or drag them around in my heart like a spiritual version of the Ancient Mariner's big, dead bird. Instead, knowing myself in the Step Four sense meant forming a balanced picture of who I am and what I have to work with in this life. This necessitated—*duh!*—including my good points.

The other change in attitude I used was to detach myself and make the whole thing into a literary exercise. I love words, I love to write, and I make my living as a broadcast journalist. Therefore, instead of soul searching, which tended to make me jittery and lead to those flowery doodles, I used tools with which I was more comfortable. I sat down once more, got out my list-making material, then reared back mentally and looked at myself—at this Martha person—with my journalist's eye, as though she were a character whose story I was trying to tell. And lo and behold, a pretty good first inventory went down on paper! I'd been able to assess my character with admirable detachment.

So What, Exactly, Was the Difference?

The difference was that I had discovered a way to tell my pride and ego to take a hike. Making my character inventory into a literary exercise had taken all the judgment out of the process. I no longer felt the need to be defensive about what I wrote down, or to feel as though I had to justify myself for being who I am. I no longer felt any pressure to feel good or bad about the Martha person on that piece of paper.

It was such a relief to be able to relax for a moment and stop trying so hard to believe that, underneath the mistakes and the baloney, I was wonderful. The simple truth emerged: I am what I am. Before using my detachment gimmick, my brain had been immobilized by the conflicting pressures generated by the really cool person I wanted to be and the jerk I was afraid I was. Both had clamored to be the one put down on paper.

Getting to Know Me

We hear a lot today about improving self-esteem. High self-esteem appears to be considered a very good thing to have. Low self-esteem appears to be cause for immediate and great worry. If you're caught with low-self esteem, it's obvious to everyone that you're in even worse shape than you'd ever imagined.

I'm not exactly sure what people mean anymore when they talk about self-esteem. I remember that, before I began working the Steps, I considered high self-esteem to be tied somehow to my ability to hold my head up and bluff my way through whatever came at me. In those unsettled days, in my heart of hearts, I was desperately afraid of some psychiatrist or guru hinting that my self-esteem might be a tad on the low side, immediately qualifying me for lifetime membership in the Losers' Club.

How about you? How do you feel right now about your self-esteem? Got any? Do you sometimes feel somewhere deep inside you that having more of it might be the real key to becoming all you want to be? That, if only there were a pill you could take to boost your self-regard, then you could strut through life like Tyra Banks striding down a runway in her underwear?

For most of my adult life before Stepdom, I think the fear of being caught with low self-esteem hovered around my psyche in much the same way a small child can fear being surprised by the toilet monster. I remember feeling tremendous pressure to present myself to the world with this bright, I'm-okay-you're-okay attitude—which is fine if you're really okay. But what if you're not?

I don't know how you feel right now, but in my pre-Step days it took a lot of energy to talk myself into believing I was even close to okay. And even when I felt okay, even when I was able to strut with the best of them, I never felt peaceful and whole. My self-esteem might have been pumped, but it was on ego-steroids. Any strength I got from that kind of self-esteem wasn't for real. It couldn't have been. How could I have really *esteemed* myself, when I didn't even *know* myself? Avoiding the truth had made complete nonsense out of any relationship I had with me.

Whatever self-esteem really means, I do know it can't be built on bluff. *If you want to feel okay about yourself, you have to know the person you're dealing with.*

There's just no way to get around standing naked in front of that mirror.

The Mechanics of My Step Four

As to how I got down to business, I had two columns, one for that Martha person's strengths and one for her weaknesses. For Step Four inventory purposes, I wasn't interested in the consequences of those strengths and weaknesses, just in the strengths and weaknesses themselves. My first successful strength inventory was simply a list of the qualities within me that I liked. I wrote down something like "smart, curious, kind, independent, not a scaredy-cat, likes people, loves my daughter and Charlie." Staring at this list kept me from lapsing into the easy, luxurious escape of self-loathing. *Working the Steps is as much about accepting our areas of competence as it is about admitting our mistakes.*

The list of weaknesses doesn't have to be long, and I made mine ridiculously simple. I wrote down, "angry, obsessively sad, self-destructive, not always truthful, impatient, and too impulsive."

There I was—not so bad as I'd feared, not as wonderful as I'd fantasized. But I was real at last. On the whole, the picture of me that emerged was rather a pleasant relief. The Step Four inventory had removed the scourge of my fear of the unknown. It was an unexpected comfort finally to take an accurate look at myself.

Like all the Steps, I occasionally wander back through Step Four, although usually not in a very organized fashion. Modifications to my list show up at the weirdest times—in the shower, walking to the gym, or waking up in the morning.

It's as though a tiny light goes on in my brain that shines on some part of me that's been in darkness for a couple of decades or so, and I realize, oh, so that's how I really am! I then make a mental adjustment to my Step Four list and get on with my day. It's knowledge that's in there when I need it.

Part of the magic of the Steps is that the longer I work them, the less interested I am in thinking about myself. In fact, I get quite bored thinking about myself these days. I'm more interested in other people, my job, my cats, or my gardens. It's lovely not to be constantly digging around in my own psyche. It's lovely not to be making constant promises to myself that, from this moment on, I will get better at this or stop doing that. These days, I pretty much go with what I've got in terms of organizing my life, my time, and my ambitions. I try to do things that use my strengths and stay away from situations I know I can't handle very well. It's called self-acceptance, as opposed to self-esteem. It begins with self-knowledge and that, for me, began for real with a successful Step Four.

No Performance Anxiety Allowed!

The key words in Step Four are "honestly" and "fearlessly," and they are integral to the accuracy of both lists. My advice to you is to keep it simple. Don't dramatize. Instead, be calmly curious. Look at yourself as rationally and objectively as you can, and simply size up what you see. The challenge of the strengths list is to own fully what you do well. No blushing or false modesty allowed. The challenge of the weakness list is not just to run through your usual litany of self-doubt and recriminations, but to figure out what the root impulse is behind all the dumb, dysfunctional things you do. And you cannot blame other people. You cannot write down, "I'm defensive because I had a hard childhood." That is for therapy, not for Step Four. This list, right now, is between you and you. Write it down, read it back, and see if it fits. Take some risks. The object is to break through all those layers of self-deception and defensiveness that have taken you years to build. Be gentle and patient with yourself. Give it time. Just don't sell the process short. If the list doesn't seem right, keep trying.

Over the years, Alice has helped me clarify my Step-Four inventory. Remember, there is no final, perfect list. Initially, I think I went at my own character inventory as though it were a Trig problem—full of confusing sines, cosines, and tangents. There was only one right way to solve the problem, and I had no clue what it was! This rigid, perfectionist viewpoint gave me a weird performance anxiety. I obsessed so much about getting the list perfect that it became a great excuse not to get started! After all, this was an excuse that had worked well with me about my math homework.

This was where Alice came in. With her help, through those calm, quiet moments in her company, I began to grasp that humans are fundamentally different from Trig problems. I was a work in progress, and I was trying to work on that progress. Actually, I wasn't so much working on that progress, as collaborating on it. It was Alice and I on the road, together at last. She really was my partner in this. I cannot emphasize enough in these pages how comforting I find it to have God as a buddy, not as an awe-inspiring entity I have to figure out how to approach before being allowed access.

Keep It Simple

Eventually, as I've said, I wrote something down. Then I waited a few weeks or a few months and tried again. I had a lot of conferences with Alice about taking the whole thing less seriously. Then I looked at the list and tried again. I'm still working on this Step. I'll always be working this Step.

Let me emphasize, one more time, that I'm not talking about therapy here. You may realize you nag because you were hounded as a kid, but "I nag" is where you stop as far as Step Four is concerned. You don't have to rummage around in your childhood and find out why you are controlling. By all means go to a therapist, take Prozac, do whatever helps. This is a spiritual program, not a self-help program. Self-help enables you to understand what you can do about your problems *on your own.* Working the Steps is about quieting the din in your head so that you can hear the still, small voice of God, and, in doing so, gain strength and a productive peace of mind. For me, working the Steps brought an ability to think, feel, and behave as my best self—an ability that was beyond the harnessed willpower of self-help or the enhanced understanding of therapy.

You are ready for Step Five as soon as you've stopped worrying about the consequences of your character strengths and defects, and recognized the strengths and defects themselves. Metaphorically speaking, this happens as soon as you are able to stand naked in front of the mirror and shake hands with yourself.

One More Story

I used to do a lot of small-time theater—summer stock, repertory, community, university, street, improv, radio drama, you name it. For a long time, if I wanted to feel good about myself, I summoned the way I felt taking my bow during a run of *The Prime of Miss Jean Brodie*. I was Miss Jean. The play ran for six nights in a six-hundred seat auditorium in front of a fairly sophisticated audience. Every night but one, six hundred people rose to applaud my performance as I took my bow. This never happened in that particular theater unless the show was some big, gaudy musical. No serious actor's performance ever got a standing ovation.

It's still a wonderful memory. I'm glad I nailed old Jean and gave her the prime she was due. But thanks to working the Steps and to Alice's company, this memory no longer floats my boat. That standing ovation was, after all, for a performance. What floats my boat these days is real life. I am what I am, and today, I really am okay.

THE KICK START

- In which area of life do you have the most difficulties? Work? Home? Health? Relationships? Write them down. Be as specific as you can.

- In what ways do you excuse or justify each behavior to yourself and others? Write them down on another sheet of paper.

- Look at the excuse list and ask yourself, "Do I really want to change these behaviors?" If the answer is yes, take the excuse sheet and rip it up. Silly symbolism? Perhaps, but remember that you really do want to change these behaviors and then shred away. These are your struggles; own them! Forget about those excuses! You are after a clear look at *how* you are, not *why*.

- Now take the weakness list and locate the weak spot in your character that is behind each difficulty. For example, if you have constant trouble with co-workers, you might discover that you are jealous of their successes.

- Take a fresh sheet of paper. At the top write "Character Assessment." Draw a vertical line down a sheet of paper. On one side of the line make a list of your character defects. For example, going back to that hypothetical trouble with your co-workers' success, you would write down "jealousy." And don't worry about your co-workers' part in your problems at all. This is you learning about you.

● Now do the exact same thing for your areas of success. You may certainly start with your successes if you wish.

○ Write down your areas of strength, just as you did your areas of difficulty.

○ Write down how you usually explain your accomplishments in these areas. If you wrote down, "consistently do well in school," you might usually excuse it by saying, "I have my father's brains," or "other people gave me a lot of help," etc.

○ Rip the excuse sheet up. No excuses allowed in Step Four! These are your successes. Own them the same way you owned your difficulties.

○ Now locate the character strength behind each of your successes. In the aforementioned example, it would simply be "I'm smart." Write that down on the other side of the vertical line drawn on your "Character Assessment" list.

5

Telling Nothing But the Truth

Step Five

I WILL FACE MY MISTAKES. WITHOUT
DECEPTION OR MAKING EXCUSES, I WILL
ADMIT THEM TO MYSELF, THE GOD OF MY
UNDERSTANDING, AND ANOTHER PERSON.

We have begun a gentle but exacting process of self-scrutiny. During Step Four we examined the basic components of our character. Now we begin to concentrate on the defect side of our Step Four character component list—all those deeply ingrained parts of us that are responsible for our screwups. Please, do keep your Step Four asset list close at hand. If you begin to wallow in self-doubt or self-pity, remind yourself of your good points and snap out of it! Let me say once again that self-knowledge is wonderful and liberating, but self-pity is a big, fat waste of time!

Another Humbling Revelation

I found Step Five enlightening, but uncomfortable. While plodding through it, I uncovered a lot about myself that I'd hidden for years. While self-knowledge eventually liberates us, acquiring it is not always a lot of fun.

For example, it was while doing Step Five that I realized I kept score in relationships. If I did anything for someone out of the goodness of my heart, then deep down in an unacknowledged, fetid part of that same heart, I felt they owed me. And if I wasn't paid back in a reasonable length of time, I ticked off a red mark in my Little Black Book of Relationships and allowed myself to begin harboring resentment toward the person who'd been so remiss in the payback department. Of course, I never openly acknowledged that resentment, even to myself. But it was down there, stewing away inside me, changing that relation*ship* into a tippy, unstable relation*boat*. In other words, I valued other people to the extent that they proved to me I was valued in return. I don't think I fully trusted anyone.

Part of the problem for me was that I made friends easily. Or, perhaps, I should rephrase that and say I attracted people easily. As a result, I usually had a choice about whom I spent time with. If any particular relationship became too complicated, I could easily let it go and quickly form another with someone else. This is not a pretty picture, I know, but I think it's a fairly common practice in our speedy American lives. The world is indeed—thank you, William Wordsworth—too much with us. We're way too busy, stressed, and pressured by issues of "getting and spending." We don't have time anymore for what we see as entanglements. Or, perhaps, we just don't want to *take* the time. Sometimes I think the real reason we carry cell phones is to keep from getting in too deep with the person we're actually with.

For me, one cost of relationship hopping was that, for a decade or so, I lost the gift of loyalty. If someone hurt me, made me mad, disappointed me or made me feel unappreciated, I left them behind. I hung out with someone until either their clay feet or mine began to muddy the surface of the relationship, and then it was time to switch partners. I changed husbands, jobs, lovers, friends, and cities. All aspects of my life were fluid, still in play. Over the years, I let go of people I really valued rather than face either their shortcomings or my own—both of which are bound to come into play if you spend enough time with anyone. I'm sure even Mother Teresa required some tolerance and understanding from her cohorts.

Another cost of relationship hopping was that I lost the great comfort of having true intimacy with anyone. Instead, I had a kind of glossy, compulsive openness with everyone. There was no one person I really knew better than any other person. I was so defensively image-oriented in those days, that there wasn't a lot of the real me present in any of my relationships—including my first two marriages.

It's humbling to admit, but in those pre-Step days, I stayed so busy working on a *persona*, I didn't have a clue who I really was. I believe now that true self-knowledge, followed by true self-acceptance, is the only way into a world of relaxed, genuine intimacy with other people.

How about you? Ask yourself how, if you don't know and accept yourself, how can you know and accept another person in any way that approaches true intimacy? I think you'll figure out pretty quickly that you can't. If you hide from yourself, you're condemned to a life of comfortless solitude, no matter how many affairs you have, or how big the crowd is around you.

Coming Out of Hiding

Step Five asks us to take the great risk of knowing and accepting ourselves *as we really are*. It asks us to level with ourselves, our God, and another person about our true selves. It challenges us to join the human race as an equal among equals, viewed in our own hearts as neither better nor worse than our colleagues. It dares us to become comfortable among other people exactly as we are.

To pull this off, we have to let other people *know* us as we really are. Step Five is a big part of that process. This is the point in the Steps where we begin to deal specifically with all the truths we've hidden from ourselves and others. For me, this felt like coming out of hiding. It was scary. I don't think I could have done it without Alice's good-humored comfort and company.

I know it's a bit of a cliché, but we really are only as sick as our secrets. Secrets corrode our hearts, undermine our ability to accept ourselves as we are, and cripple our ability to connect with each other. The longer we keep things secret, the more removed we become from our true selves, and the more removed we become from everyone else. The person who feels alone in a crowd has lots of secrets. I know that for a fact, because I did.

It's paradoxical, perhaps, but silly secrets can do as much damage as serious ones. For example, I think my two most carefully guarded secrets until a few years ago were my night in jail, which was pretty serious, and the fact that I once laughed so hard during a dance rehearsal that I peed on stage in full view of an entire cast. I think I talked about my night in jail long before I talked about my incontinence. Of course, it was ridiculous to think I'd kept this a secret in the first place, because twenty people had been watching when it happened! But I still couldn't bear to talk about my public peeing to anyone, and so the memory of it sat inside me and slowly gained power, until it sometimes seemed like the one thing I'd done that truly defined me. Once I'd confessed this dreadful secret, I was surprised to find how funny the whole thing seemed, even to me. If there's anything people can understand about each other, it's our most embarrassing moments.

The Fine Print

Let me be clear about a couple of things here. The first is that you may be toting around some shared secrets. Nothing in this Step means you are allowed to spill someone else's personal, painful beans to a third person just to make yourself feel better. However, if you can spill your part and leave the other person anonymous in both name and relationship to you, then spill away. Or you can just write your part of the secret down, speak to God about it, and stop there.

The second point I'd like to be clear about is that I think each of us deserves a private life. I'm not suggesting Step Five means you blab everything to everybody. What I suggest you do is tell each of your secrets to another person. I've told you two of my most closely guarded secrets to show you the corrosive nature of secrecy, but there are plenty more I'm not going to blab about in this book. With respect, most of my secrets are still none of your business, just as your secrets are none of mine. We're after intimacy with our close friends and family, not a new career as a stand-up comedian playing our lives for laughs.

As extroverted and uninhibited as I am, I had done a lot of things that, for years, I couldn't bear to think about, let alone talk about. These secrets hadn't necessarily harmed anyone else, but keeping them was certainly harming me. And the longer I held onto them, the more power they gained. They kept me uncomfortable with myself and other people.

Step Five was my way through this discomfort. I'm willing to wager the ever-escalating cost of a tank of gas that you, too, have some corrosive secrets that are causing you great discomfort. Now is the time to find them, drag them out of hiding, and see how they look in the clear light of Step Five.

Getting to Work

The first two parts of this Step are relatively straightforward. My own progress was a bit disorganized, but it eventually evolved into writing down all my past failures and embarrassments that I didn't like to think about. I put down each time I felt as though I'd avoided responsibility. I dragged out all the times I'd spun the truth to myself about my own actions or feelings. I dug deeply into my huge stockpile of humiliating incidents, big disappointments, and prevarications, as well as all the small hustles I'd attempted to pull off on myself and others. It took a long time. It was a long list. When I finished it, I read it aloud. Then I sat down and invited Alice to listen while I read it aloud again.

The third part was more complicated. To do it, I had to trust other people. This collided head-on with my habit of scorekeeping in relationships. For once, I didn't need to talk with someone who thought I was wonderful. Instead, I needed to talk to someone who wouldn't mind my admitting I was, at times, quite *un*-wonderful.

If you are like I was when I did this Step, you'll look around at your current inventory of friends and find there isn't one of them that you feel you can trust with the whole truth about yourself. Be honest. Think about it. Isn't it accurate to say that there isn't a single person in your life whose discretion, reasonableness, and tolerance enables you to feel safe doing all of Step Five with them? Perhaps if you go to church, you feel you can trust your pastor and could talk with him or her about your childhood. But could you talk with him or her about your sex life? Perhaps you can talk about your sex life with your best friend, but how would he or she react if you sat down and let loose a couple of the things you did in the past that still bother you? What if the person you tell some of this Step Five stuff to gossips? What if he or she judges? What if he or she wants nothing more to do with you because it's too big a responsibility to know you as you really are?

About Trust

Before Step Five, I thought trust was something other people had to give to me, before I could be expected to take a flyer and trust them in return. Another person simply had to go first in the reliability department. I had to know all about them before I would drop my guard for an instant.

This was because almost everyone in those days got The Martha Show, not the real Martha. I was always mixing up self-image with reality. I enjoyed thinking of myself as trust-worthy, but I was really uncomfortable with the intimacy required to trust another person in return. I was living my life behind a one-way mirror: I can see all of you perfectly, but you can only see as much of me as I choose to reveal.

After doing Step Five, I was surprised to find that trust is a lot like love—I benefit from it the most when I give it freely to other people. This doesn't mean I trust everyone, and it certainly doesn't mean I don't get burned occasionally. But I firmly believe I am more damaged by withholding trust from everyone than I am from occasionally being fooled or betrayed. Why? Because when I tell my secrets to someone else, I'm airing out my own heart, and, as any serious housekeeper knows, a good airing is what an enclosed space needs to become happily habitable.

We Aim for Progress, Not Perfection

I don't claim to be logical about either my life or the Twelve Steps, but I am dogged. I was much less formal about this last part of Step Five, probably because I felt overwhelmed by the thought of doing it. Also, it took some time for all my deeply hidden secrets to swim to the surface. I ended up telling different secrets to different people at different times, which I still think was perfectly all right. The point of Step Five is to level with yourself about yourself. The way to be sure you're really doing this is to tell your God and one other person. You don't have to do it with style; you just have to do it!

I bumbled through my first Step Five years ago, and yet I had another secret bite the dust just last month. This particular secret had been a pain ball growing inside me for twenty-five years. Up until the moment I let it go, I'd thought it was something I wanted to keep private. It had been known only to Charlie, my daughter, and the other people involved, and it had sat inside me as a dull ache for years. Then, out of the blue, I found myself telling it to some other women. How do I feel now that I've told people outside my immediate family? I feel remarkably clean inside. I can grieve freely now for what I did instead of just trying not to think about it. I can accept Alice's usual, evenhanded, low-key forgiveness. Even more amazingly, I can now forgive myself. Again, as my Buddhist friends say, we all do the best we can at any given moment. At that moment twenty-five years ago, I wasn't doing very well. The important thing for me to remember is that I'm able to do better now.

Your Turn

I suggest you tackle Step Five as I did; take the risk of writing down your painful, private secrets and reading them out loud. Then conduct a formal session with God and tell all. Finally, whenever you feel the urge to do so, tell each secret to one other person. As every good Catholic knows, confession is good for the soul. But then, this is not exactly the same as confession. There's no theology involved here. There's no defined list of sins you need to talk about. There's no priest behind a grate telling you what to do to expunge your record. The only way you will know what secrets you need to tell someone is that you're uncomfortable hiding them.

It will help to turn off your cell phone, turn off your pager, turn off the TV, and get a good grip on a big handkerchief before you begin writing down your secrets. When you're finished writing, read them aloud to yourself and your God. If you have no person you can easily bring yourself to talk to about something, then go to an open meeting of any Twelve Step group and ask any experienced Stepper if you could confess something. Anyone at the meeting will understand. Sit down in one of those awful metal chairs and tell this person your secret. It'll take about two sentences and one minute. Don't apologize; it's who you are. Just listen to yourself say those words out loud, "I cheated on my college entrance essay by copying a friend's." You may not ever tell anyone else. But you'll have detoxified a secret that was making you sick in some way. Watch how you feel over the next few weeks. If you're like me, you'll experience a relaxation inside that feels both peculiar and tremendously welcome. Somehow, when you're telling another person about yourself, simply and without explanation, defensiveness, rationalization, or apology, it brings the real you into much clearer focus.

Fear is your biggest enemy here, curiosity is your greatest ally, and humor is your best friend. The point is to get closer and closer to being comfortable with your past and yourself.

Blabbing Your Way to Peace of Mind

Start talking. Talk to yourself, to your God, and to another person whom you can risk trusting. It will do you spiritual good. If you make a bad choice of confidants and that person spills the beans, so be it. Cross them off your list of confidants. The point is a) to get to know yourself by facing and accepting responsibility for your past actions; and b) to give a few other people a chance to get to know you better. How the world reacts to the real you is the world's problem, not yours. Keep your chin up, keep chatting with your God, and get on to Step Six. That one's a real doozy.

THE KICK START

- What are your secrets and your transgressions? What are you ashamed of about yourself? When you lie, why are you afraid of the truth? Why have you let other people down? What are the kinds of things you've done and thoughts you regret? List both actions and thoughts.

- Include anything you've done or thought that you may have already "sort of" told someone, but that still hangs around lumpishly inside you as though it were untold. Be concise and specific.

- Don't judge yourself or your list. There are no silly or heinous secrets in the context of the Steps.

- Have a formal meeting with your God and blurt out your list.

- Whom do you feel close to? If you feel close to different people in different ways, make a list and write down what you feel comfortable discussing with each person. Arrange to tell each person the things on the list you've designated for them.

6

Letting Go of the Old

STEP SIX

I WILL BE TRULY WILLING TO CHANGE.
I WILL RECOGNIZE THAT CHANGE,
EVEN FOR THE GOOD, IS NOT
COMFORTABLE, BUT THAT FEELING
UNCOMFORTABLE IS NO EXCUSE
TO KEEP SCREWING UP.

It seems to me the process of screwup recovery happens in stages. In the beginning, we simply grit our teeth and stop doing whatever we're doing that makes us unhappy. This part roughly correlates to withdrawal in kicking a substance abuse habit, and it lasts a relatively short time, depending upon how ingrained the habit has become within us.

Based on my own experiences with substance abuse, this is also the easiest part of the whole process. Why? For me, it's because I was *doing* something. I was fighting the good fight, as the old hymn says, which is fun for someone who has a broad streak of the Can-do Kid in her character.

I think the same thing holds true when it comes to any behavioral habit or thought that gets in the way of peace of mind. This is the willpower part of the change process. It's like Lent or a bet with a friend about giving up chocolate. Anyone can give up anything for a short period of time when we're powered by the cleansing energy of self-denial. And I do not mean to imply that is not an absolutely necessary part of the process. Obviously, the first thing any of us has to do to change a behavior is to take a deep breath and stop doing it.

But, as I found out again and again, using self-denial to stop a behavior for a certain length of time is not the same thing as changing that behavior. I've learned through sad and frustrating experience that, if I simply stop doing something dumb or unhealthy, the urge to behave or think in that same stupid way doesn't disappear.

I think it's fair to say I've proved this hypothesis. I cannot count the number of times I've gritted my teeth and stopped doing whatever I was doing that was making me unhappy at the moment. I'd behave perfectly for a week or two and then, being silly and naive, I'd think, "There! I've got that licked!" But the impulse toward that ill-advised behavior was still a part of me, as strong and controlling as ever. And so one day—sometimes even without any conscious decision on my part—I was back at it, going at my bad habit at a full-tilt boogie. Substance abuse, petty lying, losing my temper—you name it. When this happened, it always felt as though some possessive devilette had patiently bided her time until my guard was down. Then she'd pounced and taken her territory back.

These failures triggered varying degrees of despair. Whenever one occurred, I'd experience a moment when I'd feel separate from myself. I'd watch this dingbat relapsing yet again, feel her panic, and think, "How the hell did *that* happen? I don't want Martha to behave like this. I don't remember giving her permission to behave like this." At this point, I had to face the fact that not only was I not running *the* show, I wasn't even running my *own* show. There appeared to be some kind of psychic override in my system that had taken over and sent me toddling off in full screw-up mode again.

After trying and failing, again and again, I realized I could not expect to deal with any of my bad behaviors in the same stupid way and have the results be more successful. So much for teeth gritting and willpower being the final solution to that particular problem. Evidently it was not going to be enough just to command myself to stop. That was not going to lead to any real change. After this depressing realization, the issue at hand became not so much how to stop screwing up, as how to rid myself of the *compulsion* to screw up?

Well, I thought, got me. I don't have a clue.

It was back to Step One—*déjà vu* all over again, thank you very much, Yogi Berra. I had recognized my complete powerlessness over yet another part of me.

What's the Point of All This?

Looking ahead, the last part of really changing anything is Step Seven—requesting that such a change occur. Step Six, the one you're on right now, is where you get ready to do that.

"Duh," I thought, when I first read Step Six. "This is ridiculous. I've been ready to stop being so angry, sad, self-destructive, impatient, and impulsive my whole life. Let's just get on with it!"

Of course, what I'd been ready for all those years was a magic wand, not a spiritual program. The general lack of magic wands is probably why Step Six uses that confounded word "willing." It states that we have to be *willing* to change before we can *begin* to change. And the truth was that I wasn't willing, not in the least.

For example, my personal tape loop of sorrow would play in my head, and I would cuddle up to my familiar grief like Linus to his blanket. I had no real desire to let my sorrows go. If I did, what would take their place inside my head? How would I even know it was *my* head anymore? Or, just before I lost my temper, I'd always tell myself that I didn't want to let fly. But the truth was, I *did* want to let fly. I didn't really want to pass up such a splendid opportunity to get angry. I was *good* at getting angry. I was *comfortable* getting angry. The results were predictable. I had a familiar, weirdly satisfying feeling of control when I got angry. If it made me and everyone around me miserable, that was just the price that we all had to pay for the sweet solace of the familiar.

The truth is that I had been struggling for so long that I had *become* my struggles. On any deeper level than dutiful, wishful thinking, I really didn't want to change. It was more disquieting to contemplate the strangeness of feeling better, then it was to cling to the sweet familiarity of feeling bad.

It's the same for you, isn't it?

The unsettling reality for most humans is that change—even change for the vastly better—feels so uncomfortable and scary that it becomes an unnatural act. Emotionally, it's tantamount to sticking our hands in the fire; every warning system in us fights the act.

What I've slowly come to believe is that, after a certain point in our lives, you and I are mostly stuck with ourselves, and there's nothing much we can do about it. At this moment of truth you may, if you wish, take out your Step Four defect list, stare at it, and indulge in a moment of existential despair. I did. Then I had yet another conversation with my buddy, Alice, about powerlessness. "I'm stuck!" I said. "Help!"

Thaumaturgy, or the Performance of Miracles

Step Six and Step Seven are what I think of as the miracle Steps. No, I'm not talking about burning bushes, winning the lottery, or any external show of divine power. Instead, I'm talking about my good companion, Alice, changing things about me that I could not change about myself. I'm talking about having confidence that, with Alice's good company, there is a better, happier, and more peaceful way, even for me. Even for you. Even if neither one of us can see exactly where we're going.

What Step Six does is challenge us to get ready for the miraculous results of changing our behavior.

A Short Story of a Small Miracle

I like old people. I always have. My parents' friends used to talk to me at dinner parties as though I had a brain and thoughts and stories they would like to hear. In return, they would tell me their thoughts and stories. These stories always interested me, seasoned as they were with adult experience and perspective. I think what drew me to broadcasting was the opportunity it gave me to hear other people's stories. And when I'm out gathering material, it often seems that older people have richer stories and they tell them better.

I suppose it was only natural that when I was taking my first baby Twelve Steps, I was drawn to older people who had been through similarly hard times. It was a very healthy attraction. Older people were both kinder and tougher on me than my contemporaries. One old guy I met in those early days of recovery from substance abuse liked to give out little hardbound, daily meditation books to newcomers who were trying to figure out how to straighten out their lives. I didn't really want one, but I took one anyway because I liked the old guy's stories. I also liked the way that little book felt in my hand. It was built to last, with a solid buckram cover and a sewn binding. Its pages opened willingly and were not constantly threatening to fall out. This was a book made to use over a lifetime. Not that I was planning to use it at all.

Somehow the old guy's stories must have haunted me, for I found myself resolving to read his stupid little book daily for a year. I didn't expect any enlightenment from its pages. I read them purely out of respect for my elderly friend's kind, but obviously misguided, impulse to help me. I was still too egotistical to accept any real help from other people, and I was also not a meditation candidate in those early days. I enjoyed the little book's blurbs, but I was still way above profiting from any such generic assistance. It was way too one-size-fits-all for me, suffering as I was—as my friend John puts it—from terminal uniqueness.

By the end of that year, however, I'd formed a habit of reading my little book as part of my morning check-in with Alice.

So, I trudged through it for a second year. I also began to mark passages in it that struck me as simple and true and strangely relevant in my life.

By the third year, I was willing to accept there might possibly be something in its pages that I could use. I was surprised at how safe it felt to appropriate any wisdom I discovered in the little book. There was no gang of indoctrinated souls waiting to gather me in. Whatever I got out of it was freely offered, with no party line attached and no proselytizing intended. These pages had been written by kind, experienced people, and their wisdom was there for me to take or leave as I chose. In other words, I had begun to think about the possibility of learning from what other people had to say about getting through the day, about God, and about working the Steps. I no longer *had* to scoff at other people's ideas about living, simply because they were not my own.

Many years later, I'm still reading that little book on most mornings. It's like working out; I can skip a day now and then, but I've found that if I skip too many, I begin to feel out of sorts. I miss communing with it, for, as the years have marched by, my understanding of each day's page has shifted and deepened.

So why am I going on and on about the little book? Because it says something important about miracles that I didn't get *at all* the first couple of times I read it.

Webster says miracles are "an event or effect in the physical world deviating from the known laws of nature, or transcending our knowledge of these laws." For me the Miracle of the Little Book is that I, Miss Independent, learned through its gentle power to be willing to change. I became open to input from other people. Through reading that book, I came to value a whole mindset I'd once considered dreck. And that, for me—as belligerently independent and intellectually arrogant as I'd always been—is a miracle.

Alice, Doing Her Thing

According to the old man's little book, all true miracles occur in the human heart, and all true miraculous work is done through people. When I first began working the Twelve Steps, I thought all this palaver about a miracle happening in a human heart meant they happened in *other* people's hearts. Surely, my new pal Alice realized that I was fine, and so she would naturally get busy changing all the people who annoyed the hell out of me. I fully expected her to work things so that the next time I ran into these people, they would be much pleasanter for me to deal with. Quite simply, I thought that when it came to miracles, I got to be Alice's boss. I thought that if I was a good girl and tried very hard to be agreeable and pleasant and to tell a close approximation of the truth, then I would be allowed to call the shots about who changed and how.

I firmly held onto this presumption through the first three Steps. Then I ran smack up against Steps Four and Five. Initially, I did these as casually as I did everything in those first days of stepping, but I still managed to recognize my part in the interpersonal brouhaha that I was calling life. Not that I saw everything wrong as my fault, but I did, at least, become able to accept myself as a willing perpetuator of my own unhappiness.

From this it was a short unpleasant stumble to the realization that my ability to change anything began and ended with my own behavior. Other people's behaviors were theirs alone to change, or not to change, as they saw fit. It still makes me rather anxious to think about this, because it means I can't ever count on anyone else coming around to my way of thinking. I can't ever count on anyone else changing at *all*. What a complete and dreary drag that was to contemplate!

It's taken me years, but I've finally gotten the message—from the little book, from working the Steps, from listening to other people's stories, and from looking back over my own life—that *my behavior is the one entity I can expect to change.* Of course, as I know from sad experience, I can't even do that by myself. For my behavior to change, it's going to take a miracle worked in *my* heart and in *my* mind.

Okay, Alice! You're on!

My Part of the Process

I found out that I was not without responsibilities in the miracle proceedings. Before Alice could do her thing and expunge my hair-trigger temper, for example, I had to allow myself to be truly curious about what it would be like to feel differently—that is, what it would feel like not to be my old self anymore. My quick, defensive temper was like my favorite old shoes, battered, beaten, worn through at the toes, and ground down at the heels. Everyone else was sick of seeing them on my feet, but to me they were comfortable and familiar. I had to muster considerable courage to hand the old clogs to Alice and trust that she would help me find something new to walk around in.

This willingness stuff—being willing in the Step Six sense of letting go of all attempts to control other people, places, and things—was scary at first. It can still be scary, even though now I do trust the process for the most part. At the beginning, however, I felt that, by putting all my trust in some newly embraced, invisible, intangible "God of my understanding," I was launching myself on a blind journey into the unknown. It made me feel as though—thank you, Paul Simon—Julio and I were *still* stuck down in the schoolyard and *still* didn't have a clue where we were going.

Before I entered Stepdom, I was completely results-oriented in every aspect of my life. I liked to see direct evidence that I was doing something worthwhile with my time. For example, years ago, when my finances were a mess and I was struggling hard to zoom up to a net worth of zero, I took a job selling cars. It was Hell on Earth for me. My job was to sit caged in a mostly empty showroom for eight or ten hours a day. Once I'd mastered the nuances of torque, there was nothing for me to do 80 percent of the time. My cohorts watched golf on television while they waited for customers. I tried, but I've never been able to get into regular daytime television. Management didn't allow you to read. They thought it looked unwelcoming to customers.

It was the worst job I've ever had, and I was absolutely no good at it. I got fired after a couple of months because I'd only sold two cars. My point? I hated that job mostly because it ran on other people's timetables. It robbed me of feeling in control, of being the one to decide what I wanted to accomplish, of planning how I was going to do it, and of deciding how long I was going to take making it happen. In order to earn a living selling cars, you must have enough patience and enough faith in the process to sit around and wait until a customer decides to show up. In those days, I had the patience and faith of a nervous flea.

Back to Being Willing to Change

As I began to contemplate the possibility of behaving differently, I found I wanted to control *that* process, as well—or at least the results of that process. I didn't want to let go of any comfortable bad behavior without being allowed to pick the charming new behavior that would take its place. I might give up my old shoes, but I certainly expected to be allowed to pick out the new ones. I wanted to be able to order up my new improved character the same way I ordered food at McDonalds. *Supersize your new peace of mind? Why yes, thank you very much!*

This is where faith comes in. Being "entirely ready to experience the miracle of change" is one more component of having faith. The truth is you and I have no control over any change in our lives that comes through working the Steps. I didn't have any idea how a less irritable Martha would get through her days, assert herself at work, relate to her friends—or her cat, for that matter. But, as familiar and as comfortable as the old pepper-pot Martha was, I'd finally gotten sick of being her. I was sick of hurting other people. I was sick of chaos. I was sick of living a life that took so much repair work. I'd tried every kind of willpower, therapy, and self-help I could find, and none of them had worked for long. And so, at last, I became truly willing to change. The paradox of faith is that we must trust in the unseen to change the seen. I had to give up the comforting myth of control, and trust in good, old Alice to do her thing with my character defects and the screwups they wrought. And to do it in her own good time.

Please remember that the Steps are not a quick fix. They are not a new "miracle" diet or exercise plan. They are not about looking good, increasing your self-esteem, or improving your efficiency rating at work. Those benefits may very well come along, but they will be side effects of the fundamental changes in you and your behavior that we're talking about now. The kinds of changes we're talking about in Step Six result in a paradigm shift deep within us. It lets us be at peace with ourselves and so, eventually, with the rest of the world.

What to Expect

In my experience, miracles of change do not arrive with a thunderclap, but they do leave a trail of bread crumbs. I recognize my own miracles by looking backwards and charting their path through my past. It's then obvious to me that something has happened in my life that feels at least as miraculous as "an event or effect in the physical world deviating from the known laws of nature, or transcending our knowledge of these laws." I can see that, over time, I've stopped being at the mercy of those character defects that had firmly controlled my life for years. I now have day after day of satisfaction. The change came quietly, in its own time, in its own way. And I think this change in my life *is* a miracle.

So what exactly do you need to do to work Step Six? Like the first three Steps, Step Six requires arrival at a state of mind rather than performance of a particular task. First, I suggest that you allow yourself to be curious about a new life in God's company. Then you have to rally sufficient courage to let this new life unfold in its own time and its own way. Yes, Captain Kirk, at last you are boldly going where you have never gone before. It takes real guts to tolerate a miracle.

THE KICK START

- What's the biggest, happiest, most fulfilling change for the better you've ever let happen in your life? Write it down. Describe all the unseen challenges it presented, the discomfort it caused, and the stress it produced. Write down how you felt, how you acted, and what you thought. If you wrote down "marriage" describe the first year *accurately*. If you wrote down "landed big promotion" or "got my dream job," describe the first year of that experience *accurately*.

- Fantastic though it was, this turn for the better in your life was tough, right? But you would do it again, right? Hang onto that experience and look forward to Step Seven.

7

Let the Good Times Roll

STEP SEVEN

I WILL TAKE A DEEP BREATH AND ASK TO CHANGE WITH ALL MY MIND AND HEART.

The first time I read Step Seven, I thought I would roll through it on greased grooves. After all, I'd done all this stressful soul searching. I knew exactly what I wanted to change about myself, and I was willing to keep the demands simple. Like Lucy in *A Charlie Brown Christmas,* all I wanted was my fair share. All I wanted was the defects side of my Step Four list expunged from my character.

Frankly, I thought I deserved a bit of a break after having anguished my way through the first six Steps. It seemed to me Step Seven should be Alice's job. All I should have to do was formally petition her to tell my bothersome character defects to take a hike. Then I would be able to sit back and relax while she got busy creating the new, defect-free me.

I did indeed ask, and Alice did, indeed, get busy. But I was somewhat startled by the "new me." She was remarkably like the old me. She just acted and felt differently about the events of her days. Step Seven hadn't been quite the character makeover I'd envisioned. I wasn't completely reinvented as a lovable saint. I'm still trying to figure out exactly what did happen inside me, and to accept that I may never know. All I can say for sure is that today I'm happy, and life keeps getting better in ways I could have never imagined.

A Progress Review

Changing your life is—like—sooooo *Promethean,* don't you think? So where are we in the process? In Steps One though Six, we've done all the necessary groundwork. We've admitted that by ourselves we're stuck behaving in a way that leaves us feeling disorderly and distressed. We've hooked up with a higher power, looked ourselves over thoroughly, then laid both our defects and strengths out before our higher power and another person we respect. We've scrutinized the mistakes we've made: the brouhahas we've engaged in, the fibs we've told, the hurtful things we've done to others and to ourselves. We've come clean about all this to ourselves, to God, and to another person. We've faced up to how complicated it is for us to change. We no longer think it's a simple matter of stopping one thing, doing another, and washing our hands of the problem. We've realized that changing for the better means giving up our comfortingly familiar excuses, anxieties, and resentments. In other words, we've prepared ourselves to be different. So now it's time to take a deep breath and actually ask to change.

Doing Our Part

Let me be clear about a couple of things. I think no amount of spiritual growth or cozying up to Alice ever means I should tell my brains and knowledge to take a hike. Neither should you. Before and after you do Step Seven, by all means go to a good therapist and take any prescribed medication that helps. Read every self-help book you can find that speaks to coping with your particular problem. Attend every support group in which you feel comfortable. I did and still do. I began working the Twelve Steps in the first place because, although all these things were helping, none of them were getting the job done. I have found Alice to be my *partner* in the miracle of change, not a Santa Claus who passes out freebies. It's quite clear to me now that, if I want to live my life well, I must take responsibility for the quality of its raw materials. I should do everything I can to stay both physically and mentally healthy. Then I am to let go of the controls and let Alice do her thing.

Slowing Down, Letting Go

As I've said before, I realized early in my relationship with Alice that I had no concept of how to get where I wanted to go, or how to move from disorder to serenity. All I knew was that, dammit, I wanted to feel better! I wanted pleasant, less stressful days. I wanted to behave in ways that made me feel good instead of bad.

Before Alice and Stepdom, I'd always supposed that any important change in my life for the better would happen from the outside. The right man, the right job, or the right therapeutic perspective on my childhood would allow me to rise above all the internal and external chaos of my so-called life. My expectations of Step Seven were way too low. I was making the miracle of change synonymous with a good analgesic, a good date, or a good book. What I really hoped was that Alice, if she were able to do anything at all, might provide me with better distraction from the mass of impulses that drove me through life. I don't think I ever expected the chaos to smooth out.

What I'd done was confuse a request for change with a request for better diversions. This went right along with how I lived back then. As my road buddy Emmylou Harris sang a couple of decades ago, "I was born to run." I courted edginess. I had a deeply ingrained reliance on distraction and entertainment to get me through the day. I had no real experience of equanimity; it was way *tooooo slooooooow.* I didn't really want to let go of the stressed-out feelings that let me know I was alive and kicking in this, the age of multitasking.

It's probably even less cool to be calm now than it was when I began working the Steps. One of the things I've noticed about our nascent twenty-first century is that it's in love with frenzy. At least in the United States, we equate clamor with glamour. We've always been the can-do culture here in America. Now we insist on doing six things at the same time, all at full volume amplified by monstrous subwoofers. *Can you hear me now?*

All this mayhem may be diverting, it may be energizing, it may make for a good buzz, but it doesn't make for peace of mind or a strong connection with the God of our understanding. And I don't know about you, but it leaves me feeling frazzled. In such a tumultuous context, quaint qualities such as serenity, composure, and quiet focus wander homeless. It's hard for them to take up residence in minds and hearts that constantly court distraction. You can't have a good buzz and equanimity at the same time.

Pushing Hard, Then and Now

Before I began working the Steps, I equated real living with pushing hard at any restrictions I faced. Such a resistant attitude certainly kept me busy and distracted for a number of years. For some people it may work for a lifetime, but such an attitude wore me out by my mid-thirties. I woke up one morning to find that everything I did, from brushing my teeth in the morning to brushing my teeth at night, took tremendous effort.

Through communing with Alice and working the Steps, I've since come to accept that my personal life is sweeter and more fun when it's about *being*, not about *doing*. I now see clearly that I have two choices: I can either take the controls and charge ahead into the frenetic world of pain and disaster, or I can take a deep breath, dig down inside to connect with Alice, and hand over the controls to her. The first is doing; the second is being. Being requires faith, but it is a lot more satisfying, a lot more fun, and it lets me sleep a lot better at night.

It seems paradoxical, but I've found that *being* requires more self-discipline than *doing*. It's easy for me to let my personal life be swept up by activities, all of which seem worthwhile or entertaining at the time. It takes a daily exercise of self-discipline to stake out the time required to slow down my mind enough simply to *be*. I also have to carve out enough time for physical rest. For me, fatigue is a compelling invitation to return to the buzzy life I lived in the bad old days. I try to avoid thinking that anything I have to do is worth weakening my connection with God. I guess my form of worship is carving out the time and the mental space it takes to maintain a conscious connection with Alice.

That said, I still push unapologetically at the boundaries of my professional life. I'm unrepentantly ambitious, not for money or power, but for challenging professional engagement. I want to earn a decent living doing something that floats my intellectual boat. When I'm working, I'm a long, tall, human Hobie Cat sailboat, keeled over as far as possible, so I can go as fast as the available winds will take me. I approach whatever I'm doing as an educational opportunity, asking what can I learn from this? How can I do this part better? What wider arena can I enter? A good day at work for me is one where I push my mental and physical limits.

Nonetheless, working the Steps has made a great difference in how I want to go about being ambitious. I hope I've become a more considerate colleague, a kinder and gentler Hobie Cat around the office. But I'm still always going to push against any kind of professional limits. That is just who I am. But, if I am decent and kind to my colleagues and tell the truth, I feel that it's okay to push myself professionally as hard and fast as I can. In fact, I feel strongly that Alice would expect no less of me.

Hanging On to Progress, Not Perfection

Okay, I'm human, and I'm flawed. I'll never do this perfectly. I'll never be able to let go of the controls completely. Please remember that I'm *slouching* toward faith, not *arriving* at it. But I do have significant amounts of time these days when Alice and I pull off a truly satisfying collaboration. I realize now that getting frustrated with someone else's behavior doesn't change them, it just puts me in a bad mood. These days I'm usually able to accept with equanimity that, when my computer freezes, I have to stop and reboot no matter how much work I've lost. My life is just as full as it ever was of misbehaving people, inconvenient circumstances, and recalcitrant technology. The *only* relevant question for me now is, am I able to accept them all with grace and good humor, and enjoy the rest of the day?

This brings me to my personal theory about the actual kind of transformation we're asking for in Step Seven. Looking back at my years spent toddling along through the Steps, I don't think my basic nature has really changed all that much—maybe not at all. While I certainly act and feel quite differently, at heart I'm still the same person I unearthed during my Step Four inventory. I'm still the same combination of stellar qualities and warts. I am still, and always will be, my innate self: a human being doing her best with what she has to work with. So what is the miracle I've experienced through Step Seven?

I can name it in three words: acceptance of reality. Mine is not always an unruffled acceptance. As Ringo Starr sang, it don't come easy for me to take the world just as it comes at me and see the people in it, including myself, as they actually are.

Yet, whatever kind of acceptance I've managed through working the Steps is probably the most significant and liberating accomplishment of my partnership with Alice. It has been the catalyst for a basic sea change in my attitude that (for the most part) has freed me from my need to screw up.

I see now that living in la-la land is what triggered all those self-destructive games I used to play with myself. For years, I was unable to accept anything difficult or unpleasant without a fight. All my screwups stemmed from my former brilliant tactic of getting through life by pretending I was a different person living in a different world.

These days, I'm usually able to embrace and enjoy the muddle of my existence and the intricacies of my character, and truly make the best of them. I'm usually okay with cheerfully plowing ahead through my day's impenetrable forest of responsibilities, tasks, disasters, successes, explosions, implosions, joys, and disappointments. Through my partnership with Alice, I've amazed myself with an unexpected ability to take the whole day as it comes, not screw things up, and accept down to my toes that this day is all I have to deal with. I may learn from the past or think about the future, but I know that one is a memory and the other is a fantasy. Today is all I actually need to deal with.

For me—the bebopping queen of action—this acceptance of reality on a gut level qualifies as a true miracle. Before Alice and I became tight, I couldn't accept a traffic ticket, let alone *life*—lived one day at a time on life's terms. And yes, I know that "one day at a time" is a platitude, but just because something is overused doesn't mean it isn't true.

Welcoming Serenity

Peace, equanimity, serenity—these were really scary concepts for me. For decades, I *was* my stress, my pain, and my battles. If I gave them up, who would I be? When I began working the Steps, I had no concept of what serenity felt like, or how anyone got through the day without agitation. I'd never done it; no one in my family had ever done it. No one at happy hour at my favorite bar had ever done it. The "happy" conversations held there were usually bitch sessions. My friends and I had all this stuff that had happened at work to get off our chests before we could begin to think about going home and facing our unsatisfying personal lives. We needed each other in order to decompress and unload the day's dramatized freight. What would we talk about if we'd sailed peacefully through the day? How would we compete in the contest of complaints?

The idea of simply letting go of situations that annoyed or worried me was probably the most radical concept I'd ever contemplated. By myself, I could never have done it. I was too committed to managing the world and too uncommitted to being my true self.

Please don't think for one moment that I am advocating tight-lipped passivity. We all have an obligation to speak up loudly and clearly whenever we think there's something fishy or wrong or cruel going on around us. We also have an obligation to face and articulate problems in personal and professional relationships before those problems have time to fester. The devil is as hard at work in sins of omission as in sins of commission. Personally, any kind of manipulative or passive-aggressive behavior makes me want to throw up.

So What Exactly Am I Advocating?

First of all, I'm advocating that I resist the temptation to tell you how to run your life, and instead simply tell you how I run mine. Every morning, when I don't forget, I ask Alice to help me find the capacity to put a sock in my big mouth and allow other people enough space to be themselves. I ask for the guts to live among colleagues and friends and look for the best in them. I ask for the curiosity to deal with these people exactly as they are and not to spend one moment of my precious time worrying about what I think they should be. And I ask for the grace to be my best self in their company, no matter what kind of a day I might be having, or how much of a pain in the ass they seem to me at the moment. Most days I come pretty close to being able to do these things. And there's no way I could have done any of them before I put in my request to Alice that we get cracking and do our thing together.

I do firmly believe what the little book says, that all true miracles of change happen in personalities and through people. Over the years, as I've noodled along through the Steps, I've certainly seen Alice rack up miracles of change in me and in my life. I've also seen other people experience such miracles in their lives. I'm happy for them, but their miracles are their business. My business is confined to having faith, staying out of my own way, working hard, and enjoying the hell out of life. I've found it takes a lot of quiet courage to allow my life to keep getting better without trying to control the process.

Not to Lose Sight of Those Screwups

I can imagine that right now you're saying something like: "Okay, Martha, I'm glad *you're* happy now, but what about all those behaviors *I* want to get rid of?"

I do realize that you want to be able to stop snacking compulsively, or nagging your children or feeling uncomfortable with your sex life—or, perhaps, the lack of it. And the only specific change I've described so far has been a trickle-down miraculous improvement that will come along sometime, as long as you give up trying to control the behavior in the first place and turn the whole mess over to the God of your understanding.

Again, all I have is my own experience. So I'm going to talk again about my old, ingrained habit of gratuitously losing my temper, which figured so prominently on my own Step Four list of character defects. As I said earlier, before Stepdom, I was usually able to concentrate my energies and stop blowing my top for a while, but the urge to explode was still always there.

My impulse toward anger was, of course, complex in origin. I'd worked on it in therapy, I'd taken prescription antidepressants, I'd stopped using addictive substances, I'd learned a lot about anger management, but I still frequently became overwhelmingly angry. And, like Old Faithful, I'd eventually erupt and scald everyone who stood too close.

Today, if I stop and think about it, I have to admit I probably still find most people annoying. I find myself annoying as well. Why can't I *ever* remember where I put my car keys? But annoying behavior, in either myself or others, usually no longer agitates me. Post Step Seven, I find I don't have to act out because of human stupidities, whether they're mine or other people's. If I'm truly angry over something, I'm able to state my feelings strongly and accurately, but those feelings no longer take over either my mouth or my behavior—at least not very often. Thanks to whatever miracle Alice got busy and worked in my personality, I'm usually able to deal with anger in exactly the same way I deal with my addiction—one day at a time. Gradually, both my addiction and my temper have lost their grip on my heart and my behavior.

I expect and hope that you will have the same experience with your most troublesome problems. I expect and hope that, by the time you've slogged your way through the Steps, you'll discover whatever you do that makes you miserable right now is no longer a compulsion. Remember, the specific outcome may not be exactly what you've envisioned when you ran the zoo on your own (thank you, Dr. Seuss), but you'll feel a lot happier with the world and a lot more at peace with yourself. This is really what you're after, right? So "let go and let God." Why not? You've tried everything else.

Alice certainly helped me clean up my act. Again, looking back at my former, spectacularly screwed-up life, I can't say that I've really changed all that much. I've still got the same Step Four list of defects and strengths, with a few additions brought by deeper understanding. However, I do see a changed life. I'm no longer defined by my stresses, my worries, or even my accomplishments. I am simply myself, and happy to be so—one rowdy, professionally charged, and personally peaceful day at a time.

THE KICK START

- The big challenge of Step Seven is to give up control of the process. Don't make the mistake of trying to peer into the future to see what will happen as you begin to change. Life will get better in ways you can't imagine. You only limit the possibilities when you try to control the journey.

- Don't underestimate the degree of real courage this Step takes. Step Seven goes straight to the heart of faith, which doesn't come all that naturally to a lot of us. Try thinking about faith as the antithesis of fear. It takes guts to stop being fearful and step into the unknown represented by any kind of change. Faith asks us to go a step further and believe that the God of our understanding, sight unseen, will take us through the process in the best way possible.

- Lighten up! Life, itself, is our greatest adventure. It's rife with possibilities, all waiting to be grasped once we chuck our fear of the unknown. It's so invigorating to take risks, especially the great and liberating risks of embracing both change and faith in God. Remember how glorious it felt as a child to try something new—such as holding your nose and jumping into a lake for the first time? Ask God to strengthen the daring that's still there inside you.

8

Oh No, Not That!

STEP EIGHT

I WILL MAKE A LIST OF THE PEOPLE I'VE HARMED AND WILLINGLY ACCEPT THAT, FOR MY OWN PEACE OF MIND, I NEED TO MAKE AMENDS TO EACH OF THEM.

I found Step Eight daunting at first, chiefly because I still clung to the Magical Thinking School of Stepping. I thought that if Alice and I partnered up and worked hard at changing me and my life for the better, there would come this magical moment when we suddenly achieved Success. When that moment came, I would simply stop screwing up, life would be fun again, and that would be that. "Mission accomplished," I would announce from the deck of my own battleship. Everybody would love me, and I'd love everybody.

You probably want to think this as well, right? In fact, you may hope that this book will help you learn to draw a line that will mark the end of the Dark Kingdom of Past Screwups, so you can step over into it into the Shining Realm of the Brand New You. One quick skip, and there you'll be—kinder, smarter, thinner, calmer, gentler, and more energetic—magically transfigured into your wildest dream of the perfect you. And of course, you'll have shed whatever grief and guilt you've been toting around from the past as easily as Angelina Jolie shed her baby weight.

Well, get a grip. This isn't a game of hopscotch. You're not going to be hopping over any neat transformational boundaries. Working the Steps is not a quick fix, just a real one. The Steps guide us through a slow process of discovery and renovation—not through an extreme makeover, á la Cinderella on ball night.

What we are doing is asking for, and accepting, help with repair work on ourselves, then allowing change to occur in ways not remotely anticipated in our own limited hopes, dreams, and plans. Let me reiterate that slogging through the Steps with Alice riding shotgun has whipped my life into far better shape than I'd ever imagined achieving on my own. It's brought me inner peace, and I'm comfortable with both myself and my past. As a result, I am free of any need or desire to wish for a Brand New Me.

Preparing My Amends List

The very first time I read Step Eight, I probably said something unprintable. What could revisiting the painful troubles of past relationships possibly have to do with staying off booze and pills, or eschewing the sweet, momentary release of losing my temper? Emotional pain had been my number one excuse for abusing alcohol and drugs and indulging my anger, and now I was expected to root around in every failed relationship I'd ever had! What good could possibly come of that? Besides, I'd already had years of therapy for the presumed purpose of salving the residual pain left over from all those bumpy past relationships. Indeed, therapy had given me understanding that brought with it some intellectual relief, but I still hurt. After going through all that, however, I had zero desire to revisit this stuff in my head. I just wanted my heart to heal.

Well, surprise, surprise! In order for that healing to begin in earnest, I discovered that what I needed to do was accept that this was pain I couldn't understand away, blame away, or, heaven knows, drink away. The big problem was that I still lugged around the burden of my own blunders *within* those relationships.

Working Step Eight forced me to get real about those blunders, to own up to how *my* screwups had affected the rocky parts of my past dealings. In order to do this, I first had to understand and accept my part in every situation in my life that had gone flooey. I had to revisit every sorry scene I could dredge up from the past that still bothered me. I won't burden you with them all. But here's a good example: the day I got fired as a magazine editor.

Taking on the Twerps

I can date my short-lived, hard-core drinking from that day. The magazine's owners and publishers were two twenty-somethings. (University of Virginia frat boys dressed up in their daddies' business suits, pretending to be business tycoons—as I scornfully termed them to myself and, probably, to a few dozen close friends.) As I remember it, the twerps had flipped a coin to decide whether they were going into the limousine business or the publishing business. Publishing had won, so they'd started a Charlottesville magazine.

I'd been its editor for over a year. During that time, I'd doubled the size of the magazine and published some truly good fiction, articles, and photography. The twerps had rewarded me with a substantial raise. I'd figured I was sailing along securely when, with no warning, they brought me into their office and fired me without explanation. I was given a choice between signing away all legal redress and receiving a nice severance package, or not signing and not getting a nickel.

I was enraged and wanted to fight, but I signed and left because I needed the money. I couldn't believe the twerps had had the nerve to fire me! They were so young, so callow, so poorly read! One of them had even admitted he didn't like to read at all, so he didn't usually make it through the magazine's articles—although he did enjoy the pictures. Here I'd made their magazine into something much more substantial, and now I was being fired! I sat in my apartment, crying and fuming, and, of course, drinking. I remember calling the twerps up and giving them my opinion about quite a few things. My night in jail was just eight months away.

The twerps didn't make my first Step Eight list. I hung onto my rage against them for a long time. It felt so righteous. A twerp is a twerp is a twerp, I told myself. How could anyone who didn't read pretend to be a publisher?! I downed a lot of bourbon thinking about this outrage before the night I went to jail. After I went to jail, I pounded out a lot of miles in my Nikes imagining all the pithy, withering things I should have said to them.

Then one fine day, after a couple of years spent working the Steps, yet another veil lifted, and I realized what it must have been like for the twerps to work with me. They'd been young, rather straight-laced, Virginia kids, funding their new business with their fathers' money. All they'd wanted was to run their publishing house the way that they wanted to. I had been quite open in my scorn for them and everything that I, in my supreme arrogance, thought they represented. I didn't really *know* them, but I'd judged them as being nonintellectual, unimaginative, and lacking in literary sophistication or knowledge. My alcohol-fueled ego had released me from any obligation to do anything they said. I'd flouted the office hours and the dress code, lost my temper frequently, and otherwise disagreed with them just for the hell of it. I'd acted as though I were editing the *New Yorker*, while all those two young men wanted was to have a pretty magazine with nice photographs and inoffensive articles that would attract the town's conservative business community as advertisers.

Even after this deflating epiphany, I continued to hold a grudge against the twerps simply because they'd fired me in such a brutal way. But my Alice-assisted clarity again intervened, and it occurred to me that those poor guys were probably scared of me. I was fifteen years older, used words like weapons, and was obviously uninhibited about losing my temper. They'd probably consulted with their daddies' attorney, and he'd advised them to get rid of me just the way they'd done it: Keep the interaction short and shocking and get her out of the building. Their goal was probably fireworks containment. Considering the way I'd acted around the office, this was probably a smart strategy.

Time passed, I hung out with Alice, life became fun again, and

I simply got tired of being mad at the twerps. They were what they were, and the truth was that my behavior had made me difficult to work with. I realized the biggest reason I'd stayed mad for so long was that they'd hurt my pride. This meant my bruised ego, not the twerps, had generated all those bad feelings I still carried around about the failure of my gig as a magazine editor.

So there it was, another chafing revelation about how my character defects had run rampant in my past. Temper and arrogance had been the driving force of my interactions with the twerps. I needed to own up to this for my own sake. At this point, I slapped the twerps (you see, I'm still no saint—I still refer to them as the twerps) down on my revised Step Eight amends list. After that, the only relevant consideration was not how *they'd* acted, but how *I'd* acted.

My past was lousy with similarly disordered relationships—as yours may be, as well. In my experience, if we want to get rid of the burden of our mistakes, we have no choice but to plow ahead through Step Eight and into Step Nine. Justifying our bad behavior doesn't relieve us of its burden. While those old mistakes cannot be undone, all those troubling incidents and their attendant burdens can be left behind. So as a small tribute to my mother, who did love her Yeats, let us arise and go now, onward to our own internal Lake Isle of Innisfree, for we shall indeed find some peace there. And the only path I've ever found to this peace is the straight and narrow one that leads through Step Eight.

Dumpster-Diving in Our Own Histories

To trot out that old truism yet again, you and I remain only as sick as our secrets. I've found that the most damaging secrets are the ones I keep from myself, so the first part of Step Eight was simply to list the painful incidents from my past that I didn't like to think about. I looked for the times my character defects had taken control of my actions. I dug up all the dark moments of conflict or outright wrongdoing for which I'd either tried to excuse myself or blame someone else.

For me, Step Eight became the "no excuses allowed" Step. It meant leveling with myself about my exact part in the tangles and pain of my past relationships—without all the side chatter about *why* I did what I'd done. This Step was the one where I started to develop a habit of accurate, but *nonpunitive,* self-assessment of my role in difficulties with my daughter, friends, colleagues, ex-husbands, and ex-lovers—even, I blush to say, with my family's cocker spaniel.

Let me add that this was also the Step where I learned to laugh at myself and not to take myself and my mistakes so seriously. This was the Step where I finally faced the bare-naked fact that I am not the center of any world bigger than the one inside my own head—and that the quality of life on that tiny Planet of Me is the only part of the larger universe over which I have any control. What I've found through experience is that the kinder, gentler, and more straightforward I am with other people, the more orderly, peaceful, and enjoyable life on the Planet of Me becomes, and the less I am compelled to act out and create disorder on either my planet or other people's.

What we do in Step Eight is clean our emotional houses in preparation for a simpler, better, happier life.

What I Actually Did

Step Eight said to make a list, so that was how I began. I worked from my Step Four inventory, breaking down my character defects into a list of specific incidents. I put down everything I had done to other people that still had the power to stir up unpleasant emotions. I did my best to be objective and honest and include every time a screwup of mine had involved and somehow damaged someone else.

But, as I quickly discovered, just because an instruction seems straightforward, doesn't mean it is easy to fulfill. It was terribly difficult for me to stop defending my own ridiculous behavior to myself. For example, I hurt my first two husbands pretty badly, mostly by making a horribly messy job of leaving both relationships. (Let me add here that both of these guys have gone on to marry perfectly wonderful women and, from the distant perspective of an ex-wife, appear to be happy.)

My old internal dialogue about those graceless exits went like this: Well, what did you expect? You were confused, restless, and adrift. They weren't helping you feel any better. That was the reason you did what you did.

On my list I simply wrote down, "Took out my own confusion on my first two husbands." Once it was written down, I could accept that they were both good guys—whom I had probably loved in my own screwy way back in the days when I was just not viable marriage material.

Paradoxically, this is also the Step where I became more confident of my strengths. Once I had written down, "Took out my own confusion on my first two husbands," I was also able to see that I had crawled out of those marriages because they weren't healthy for me, and I was determined to be healthy. This insistence on achieving health, however poorly handled at times, is one of my great strengths.

The gift of this Step was that, as I honestly accepted responsibility for my part in each past contretemps, I left guilt and anger behind. The bad parts of the past stayed put in the past and the good memories stepped forward. I remembered all the fun I'd had with those husbands once I stopped wrestling with my guilt about how I'd left them.

Yet Another List

That's how the first part of Step Eight goes. Now, it's time to move on to "willingly accept that, for my own peace of mind, I need to make amends to each of them." Yes, here we are nose-to-nose with willingness again. So what exactly does "willingly" accepting something mean?

This is where I realized that working the Steps was altering how I viewed and responded to life's troubles. This is another change I could never have achieved on my own. There was nothing in my basic, pre-Alice character that would have enabled me to stop justifying my mistakes, blaming other people for my failures, feeling sorry for myself, and generally whining and complaining. Before the Steps, I wasn't wise or strong enough to stand metaphorically naked on my own two feet and admit to myself that I'd done something wrong in the past and now felt sincerely sorry for having done it.

But why, exactly, do *I* have to be the one who admits to being wrong? If I've stolen or lied to get what I want, the answer is pretty obvious. But why, when a situation degenerates into a disaster, and its memory lodges in my past as a burden, am I necessarily the one who has to admit I was wrong and become willing to make amends?

I don't *have* to, of course. I can keep on keeping on. I can stare at my Step Eight list and get mad or grow ashamed about the incidents listed on it for the rest of my life. However, it finally dawned on me that my chief problem in thinking about the incidents on my Step Eight list was not so much what had happened, as it was the load of anger and guilt they'd generated that I was still toting around.

To reiterate another Twelve Step truism, we cannot expect to handle anything in the same way we always have and get new results. As long as we live on this earth, our days will never be tangle-free. There will always be times when we annoy, injure, or fail each other. As my father used to say, life would be so easy if we just didn't have to deal with other people. Gradually, it became clear to me that, in this life, I had a pretty clear-cut choice: either change my mechanisms for coping with bad memories or continue to feel awful.

This is another place in my slow and painful progress through the Steps where my good buddy, Alice, gave unquantifiable amounts of help. How else, but in quiet communion with her, would thoughts and impulses that I'd never had before have come to me? How else would I have become capable of simplifying the complicated burden of my own past mistakes into something I could handle?

Here's how it happened. First of all, Alice and I got my priorities straight. I was sick of feeling awful. I really did want to feel better. I wanted to have long, peaceful days go by without the horrible internal jolts triggered by anger, resentment, and self-pity. It finally dawned on me that, in order to stop feeling bad about the past, I first had to own my part in it and become willing to do whatever I could to set situations right. That's how healing begins, and that's what the second part of Step Eight is about.

In order to become willing to make amends about past mistakes, I had to entirely forget about assigning blame. I might *not* have been the only one who was wrong in any given incident, but my wrong was the only wrong I could amend. Eventually I came to realize that my wrong was also the only wrong that truly bothered me. Take the twerps, for example. The truth was that *my* part in that mess was the burden that weighed so heavily on my head and my heart. Once I stomped on my ego long enough to do some Step Eight work, that burden was speedily lifted.

What's the Pay-Off?

I always feel better immediately after I've admitted my part in any screwup. However large and cumbersome the burden, and however long I've been toting it around, it vanishes. Self-justification for screwing up is a lot of wasted huffing and puffing. It will only prolong my misery.

It was so simple to become willing. All I did was to sit quietly, take a look at that list of painful incidents in my past that I'd made in the first part of Step Eight, and ask Alice for the strength to embrace the second part of the Step.

It's your turn. You've made your list. If you're feeling reasonably relaxed, take it out, read it, and ask the God of your understanding to give you the strength to become willing to make amends for your part in those messes. What have you got to lose? If you're like me, you've already discovered that you cannot entirely let go of past pain on your own.

THE KICK START

- Remember, no self-flagellation allowed! Get a good night's sleep and pick a time when you're feeling relaxed and okay with yourself.

- Ask your God to keep you emotionally detached and objective. Take a deep breath. Focus on the past relationship that has always triggered the most anger and resentment inside you. If you're divorced or having severe problems with your current life partner, that's probably a good place to start.

- Resist the impulse to get angry and resentful all over again. Lighten up! Remember you're changing, and change is uncomfortable. The point is to move on in your life. No one but God is around, anyway, so what have you got to lose by viewing this past mess from a different angle?

- Revisit one fight with this person where you know your character defects were in control of your actions. Forget about what the other person did and concentrate on what you did. Write down anything that you feel the need to justify or explain. Don't argue with the concept, just do it.

- When your list is finished and you are ready, ask the God of your understanding for the *willingness* to make amends to the other people involved for the harm you have done them. "Willingness to make amends" means that *you are willing to forget about the other person's screwups.* "Willingness to make amends" means *recognizing that your life is more deeply damaged by what you do to others than by what others do to you.*

● Recognize that this willingness alone is a tremendous change within you. It takes uncompromising work, time, patience, a sense of humor, and *faith*. As soon as the change begins to take hold, you will feel much better about yourself and life in general.

9

Whole Lotta Shakin' Goin' On!

STEP NINE

I WILL MAKE WHATEVER AMENDS I CAN TO THOSE I'VE INJURED WITHOUT DOING FURTHER DAMAGE TO ANYONE.

Good Golly, Miss Molly! You don't mean I'm supposed to seek out all the people I've done wrong in the past and apologize to them?

Maybe, maybe not.

In other words, not exactly.

The Steps are a grand spiritual adventure. They are not a set of rules promising specific rewards if we obey them and harsh punishments if we don't. The Steps don't call for obedience to any creed. Instead, they require our best efforts assisted by God's company.

For me, this meant rummaging through my speckled personal history and airing out all the dank corners where I'd kept my pain, anger, and embarrassment. These fetid hidey-holes were not unfamiliar—I'd poked around in them a lot during my years of screwing up—but this new airing out was done with good old Alice riding shotgun. For me, Alice's company made all the difference. With her around, the past remained the past, without the spooky power to cloud the present with any of the ambivalence, defensiveness, self-pity, and bad temper that I had generated on my own.

So, once those corners were fully opened up for inspection, then what?

A New Kind of Thinking

I found that I had a surprising amount of direct intellectual input into this Step. In other words, I had to *think* again, a process the first eight Steps had trained me to minimize in favor of consultation and communion with Alice. But ever since I'd learned to stop over-intellectualizing, stopped devising creative excuses, and stopped parceling out blame, my brain had been able to assess dispassionately the wrongs I had done to other people. I found myself truly interested in determining if I could do something *now* that would amend the pain I had created in the past.

The key word during this process for me was dispassionate. Another person's well-being was the only consideration I was allowed in making amends. This was not about exhibiting my new humility for all the world to see. In fact, it was irrelevant whether making amends would make *me* feel any better. As far as my own feelings went, I would have to settle for my own and Alice's forgiveness.

I also had to tread softly and carefully. It was extremely important for me to remember that the mistakes of my past were a shared burden. I had to accept the possibility, right from the start, that not all the folks I'd wronged would want to be reminded of these experiences, even for the purpose of lightening their own hearts' load.

What to Do, *Exactly*

I had my Step Eight list, and I was able to think about the amends process clearly and unselfishly. The next thing I had to do was figure out how I should go about making my amends to a lot of different people for a lot of different reasons. What did the amends process mean? What should I actually do? The past is the past, after all. What's done cannot be undone.

With some transgressions, it was obvious. If I'd stolen something, I had to give it back. If I'd lied, I had to 'fess up unless the confession would cause someone yet more pain. But what about all those nasty fights and disagreements? What about those profitless you-said/I-said regattas?

Thinking about those pointless days of pain and rage, I slowly realized that I was not working with factual history; I was working with the myth of my own past. Of course, I'd known this all along at some level. I'd been through two divorces, seen a child through adolescence, and weathered periodic career storms. The other people involved remembered these events very differently from me. The problem for me was that, before Alice's supportive company, I hadn't had the guts to *accept* these differences. My attitude about my past painful muddles had always been, damn the torpedoes! I know I'm right! Who cares about the other person's perceptions?

But now those days of self-righteous, internal grandstanding were over. Here I was face-to-face with Step Nine, finally confident and strong enough to accept the truth: Any situation's reality is in the minds of the participants, and it's different for each player on the stage. I may have shared experiences with another person in time, but we were never going to be joined together in total agreement about what had *happened* during that time.

Once I'd accepted this, it was a short leap to the realization that making amends begins with recognizing the validity of another person's version of a shared experience. Before anything else, I had to accept that whatever I'd gone through with someone else had probably been perceived differently by each of us. I had to accept that both "truths" were equally legitimate, even though they might be very different. Whatever had actually happened between us had immediately been adapted by each of us for our own personal mythology, a saga where actual events are obscured and skewed by emotion and prior experience.

This startling realization was another gift from my second ex-husband. The man was a lawyer by training and inclination. In all our years together (during which we had a lot of fun, closeness and good times), I don't remember him ever holding a view of which he was not certain. It made me wild. Couldn't he change his mind and see things my way, just once? Couldn't he change his mind once about *something?*

I was around forty before I realized that a happy marriage is not really built upon consensus of opinion. I'm still not quite sure what it *is* built upon, but I have a very happy marriage these days, and I *do* know it's not built upon that. This is not to say I don't feel the need to speak my mind regularly to my beloved Charlie—to share my views about the vitamins he should take, for example. The difference is I just don't get bent out of shape if he doesn't agree with me, and I certainly don't feel the need to get mad about it.

Of course, another difference for me is that Charlie makes me feel as though he respects my vitamin prescription and is interested in hearing about it, even if he disagrees. He's willing to listen to my opinions and acknowledge that I might have a worthwhile thought. This gets us back to making amends. *I find that making amends to other people begins with a heartfelt acknowledgment that their version of whatever happened between us is just as legitimate as my own.*

Sometimes All It Takes Is Saying, "I'm Sorry"

A simple apology can be a real gift.

Dad apologized to me once when I was in my thirties for something enormously damaging he'd neglected to do when I was a child. To me, his apology meant he'd recognized the pain his neglect in this important instance had caused me. It was all I needed to let the whole thing slide over the edge of pain and into memory.

When I offered a simple apology to some of the people I'd hurt or offended, I could see that it was the same kind of gift for them as my dad had given me. Of course, it has to be a Step Eight inspired apology to do *me* any good. The person to whom I apologized might not have been able to tell the difference between a *pro forma* and a truly felt apology, but my own insides certainly could. I found I could not con myself *at all* when it came to faking a sense of regret. As Susanna Clark puts it in one of her great, tuneful songs, it's gotta come from the heart if you want it to work.

In my experience, anything heartfelt takes time. I had to live dispassionately with each unpleasant situation for a while before I was able to get past my own need to justify or explain. In other words, I had to examine my behavior open-mindedly from the other person's point of view—walk around in his or her shoes, as Atticus Finch puts it in *To Kill a Mockingbird*—and take the time to look back over my behavior from the other person's point of view. Only then, did I really *feel* apologetic.

Let me emphasize that I was *thinking* about the past, not *wallowing* in it, but I couldn't rush through this Step. It wasn't enough to remember every squabble in my life, spit out an apology, and figure that I was now off the hook.

Once again, if we've actually done something to someone else—stolen money, told a lie, deserted a child who was truly dependent on us—then Step Nine demands that we set things right again. If we can't do this, then we need to accept what we've done and make amends through others who were not directly involved. In some cases, the only way to do this may be by making a pledge about not repeating mistakes in the future.

Let me use my family cocker spaniel as an example. Her old age coincided with my Disastrous Years, and I essentially blew off taking good care of her. I make no excuses now. She was a truly magnificent pet, I loved her a lot, and to this day it breaks my heart to think of how she died. All I can do to make amends is to never neglect another pet. It doesn't undo my abandonment of my beloved cocker spaniel, but it does mean I no longer buy any of the excuses I had at the time for not doing a lot better by her.

Keeping Life Simple

When I was working at a small women's college, it bothered me that the culture there seemed to foster the notion in students that an adequate excuse for *not* doing what they were supposed to do was as good as actually *doing* it. This is not to say that students didn't sometimes really get sick or have true family emergencies, but most of the extensions in academic work I saw students ask for and receive were for other, much less sensible reasons. They involved a student getting too busy and simply choosing to do something else (sports, student government, or a weekend trip) rather than their academic work. I worried that students were indirectly being given the message that taking on too much and becoming frazzled was the same as being productive. Such a system fosters skewed thinking, and if such thinking becomes habitual, it will lead directly to confusion and misery.

I know this because I'd lived it. For years, I never kept my life simple and straightforward, infrequently told the truth to myself, rarely invested enough time in personal relationships, inflated my own self-importance to myself, and never saved time for adequate rest, true relaxation, and contemplation. The result was that I screwed up a lot and had to come up with great excuses for doing so.

One of the great things I've learned through working the

Steps is to accept the limitations inherent in being a human being. I've finally figured out that I can only do so much. It's no one's responsibility but mine to organize my life so that I can have the best shot at feeling good and being healthy.

Why did I honor frenetic activity so much anyway? Why do most addicts? *Webster's* defines addiction as the "process of giving oneself over to a constant practice." So an addiction is anything you feel you *have* to be doing whether it's good for you or not.

I'm one of the lucky ones who became addicted to a substance, something that society joins me in believing to be unhealthy. During my years of recovery from that substance, however, I recognized other self-destructive habits in myself at which society winks. I ran up my credit cards, ate bad food, manipulated myself and others, and multitasked myself into a constant frenzy. I had what I call the "busy-ness" addiction. I only felt alive if I was so busy I teetered on the edge of collapse. The sad part was that such frenzy robbed me of any sense of satisfaction, completion, or, a lot of the time, of feeling physically good.

So what did I think I was doing? What had kept me going at such a breakneck pace? I worked through all kinds of complex sociological and psychological explanations just to conclude that I was simply running away from Alice in favor of foxtrotting daily with some very seductive devils. I lost all sense of serenity during those years as the music played on, and I kept on dancing. The sad truth is I felt horribly lonely most of the time, even though I was busy and surrounded by people.

I have no idea why I was running from Alice. Back then, I

had plenty of excuses, but no real reason. I only know I was in the grip of tantalizing impulses that led me to do lots of stupid things. Now that I've switched partners and taken up dancing with Alice, life is simple and good and straightforward, and I feel great.

Another Cautionary Word

When I sallied forth to set everything right, I was shocked to discover that the whole world did not sit up and applaud just because Martha had finally developed the ability to behave herself. This was when I finally *understood* two of the basic truths of a peaceful and truly productive life: First, I'm not that important in the grand scheme of things; and second, I have zero control over anyone except myself.

Once again, I have my second ex-husband to thank. This poor man had evidently been so bamboozled by my years of problematic behavior that not only did he not want to forgive me, he didn't even want me to come physically close enough to him to apologize. All I wanted to do was tell him I thought he really was a good-hearted, well-intentioned guy during our marriage, and I was sorry I'd done him wrong, but he'd act as though I were trying to sell him a carton of 8-track tapes whenever I got within conversational range.

At first, I was both hurt and mystified by his stand-offish attitude. Then Alice must have removed yet another pair of ego blinders, because the day came when I looked at my motives for apologizing to my second ex-husband and thought, how grandiose is that! It had taken me a few years, but I'd finally come to the healthy realization that our relationship was simply not important to him anymore. Well, I ask you, how humbling is that?

But also how liberating! I behaved badly during my marriage to this man. I remain truly sorry about how I acted, but I've now accepted that the only thing I can do is recognize my bad behavior for what it was and try never to behave so appallingly to anyone again. And then *I must let my guilt go.* No mental melodrama is allowed when doing Step Nine!

What's the Pay-Off for Making Amends?

Well, hallelujah! After Step Nine, I finally stopped beating up on myself. I'd faced my mistakes, put right what I could, and deposited the whole mess in the past where it belonged. My arrogance was mostly gone, replaced by a truly therapeutic and liberating humility. My tape loop of sorrow and anger had finally clicked off, I'd let go of the past, and become able to turn my energy and attention to the present.

Are you inspired to get started? I do hope so. Believe me, you've got nothing to lose but your guilt, anger, and despair. However, be prepared for surprises.

When my daughter was about ten, we went on a family vacation out west. At the time we had a menagerie of finches, cats, dogs, fish, a boa constrictor, and my daughter's beloved hamster, which was left in the bathroom on the back of the toilet. We lined up a friend to take care of our zoo while we were gone.

We got back home to a pet disaster. My daughter went in to use the bathroom and let out a shriek I will never forget. I rushed in and there was her hamster, long dead and floating in the toilet. She and I huddled in the living room, leaving the man of the house to flush the hamster down the toilet without even a few words being said. My daughter was distraught.

With the help of our pet-sitting friend, we pieced together what had happened. The boa constrictor had escaped, eaten the birds, and gone hunting for more small animals. The pet sitter, who was afraid of snakes, had found the boa coiled on the screen on top of the hamster's aquarium. She had immediately slammed the bathroom door and understandably not gone in there again. The boa had then relocated from the top of the hamster's home to the bathtub, the hamster had run out of water, gotten thirsty, crawled out of its aquarium, and drowned in the toilet.

I felt guilty about this for two decades. Finally I brought it up with my daughter intending to say again how awful I felt about it—particularly about allowing the toilet flushing. I felt sure I should have fished the yucky little beast out of the toilet and given it a proper burial in the backyard. I felt sure the sound of that flushing toilet echoed to that day in my daughter's dreams and had been the subject of much discussion with her therapists.

Surprise, surprise! My daughter had no memory of the incident! She was quite amused I had worried about it so for so long. It was yet another proof that my personal memories of shared events seldom match another person's.

So, my friend, take out your Step Eight list and get cracking. Once again, there's no time limit. The healing is ongoing. Making your first round of amends will clear out some of the emotional debris you've been toting around and allow you a clearer view of the more complex, bad situations from your past.

Just the other day, I thought about something I'd done to someone and wondered if I should attempt to make amends. I consulted with Alice and decided not to. The decision was made for the other person's sake, not mine. I figured that what I'd done was simply not worth the disruption of bringing it up. After all, it had happened thirty years ago.

As Kurt Vonnegut puts it, and so it goes.

THE KICK START

- Take your Step-Eight list and pick out the simple crimes: the times you lied, cheated, stole, or consciously manipulated. Go for the events where it's obvious you were wrong.

- Decide if making direct amends to the person or persons you injured with these actions will do them any good. In these obvious cases, err on the side of boldness. If another person thinks you're stupid to apologize for lying to them in the fourth grade, so what? It does them no harm. The point is you did lie to them, and you know that you owe them amends.

- Now on to the I-said/you-said incidents:

  ○ Are you truly willing to tell your pride and ego to take a hike and accept that your version of this past event is your version *alone*? Are you willing to accept that your version of what happened is not The Truth, but only your personal memory of the experience?

  ○ Are you willing to give up blaming the other person for what happened and judging his or her behavior during the incident? (This was really hard for me. I had to ask Alice for a lot of help.)

  ○ What character defects of yours were at play during this incident? What did they lead you to do? Write this down. Whatever you did that was driven by your character defects is what you need to make amends for.

○ Step outside any anger or guilt you're still toting around. Will it do harm to the other person if you try to make amends?

♦ If the answer is no, decide how you can meaningfully make amends. Don't overlook the value of a simple apology.

♦ If the answer is yes, then figure out how you can make amends indirectly—perhaps through a kindness done to someone else.

10

Stepping Out!

STEP TEN

I WILL FEARLESSLY TAKE A DAILY LOOK AT MY THOUGHTS AND BEHAVIOR. WHEN I REALIZE I'VE GOOFED UP, I WILL PROMPTLY ADMIT IT.

One hard truth I've discovered from working the Twelve Steps is that everything I do either carries me toward a screwup or away from it. The key to avoiding screwups is not to kid myself. I must be brave enough to be honest.

Dizzy Dean, a glorious fireball pitcher in the '30s and an equally glorious color commentator in the '40s and '50s, was right up there with Yogi Berra when it came to the creative use of language. Dean specialized in slaughtering verbs. My favorite Dizzy-ism was his excited pronouncement that outfielder Al "Zarrilla *slud* into third." So, to borrow Mr. Dean's grammatical construct, if I get too casual about working the steps, I'll find I've backslud pretty quickly. The Steps are a guide to living, not a set of tasks that lead to a prize. Life along their path is a road movie, not a treasure hunt. I will never, *ever* arrive at perfection, but if I'm diligent in my working of them, I'm sure to have lots of satisfying fun along the way.

The Story of One Time I Backslud

During the years I was slow-dancing with the devilettes, anger dominated my emotional landscape. It was my first response to anything that happened that didn't make me feel good. If something made me sad, I got resentful; if somebody hurt my feelings, I seethed; whenever I was confused, I found a way to lash out. I'm sure you get the picture, and it's not one of which I'm proud.

I'm also well-aware that I've crowed in these pages—modestly, I hope, like Pooh looking down his nose—about how rare it is for me to get angry these days. It still amazes me how terribly annoying my days can become, and I don't even feel agitated. Still, I can occasionally relapse into what an old hymn calls my "sinful ways." Take the winter Saturday I was supposed to interview a moderately important person coming to our area to make a speech.

The annoyances began with the weather. It was early December, it had snowed on Friday, and Virginia is not supposed to get significant snow until after Christmas. That's one of the reasons I live here. I'm an aging beach bunny. I like hot weather and long days, summertime when the living is easy. I hate wearing a lot of clothes, wrapping my head up in things that make it itch, and not being able to strike out at a brisk pace because there's slippery stuff all over the ground. But that year, for the second year in a row, we got a real whump of a snowfall weeks before Christmas.

I spent a snowy Friday trying to find out if my interviewee was still coming. He was scheduled to speak in Charlottesville, usually sixty scenic miles from my house. On this particular Saturday, however, they would be sixty snowy and dicey miles, cutting through a mountain pass notorious for its fog shroud in bad weather. On top of that, my car had begun popping out of four-wheel drive for its own whimsical reasons.

By late Friday, no one knew yet whether my interviewee would get there. I crept home from work, slipping and sliding in and out of four-wheel drive, feeling decidedly un-serene, my plans for Saturday hung up in weather limbo. Saturday morning, I got up early and started making calls again. Around eight-thirty I found out that my man was, indeed, going to make it. By this time I had to hurry to get out the door, get to the station, pick up my equipment, and get over the mountain in time to hear my man make his speech. And so I blew off my morning conversation with Alice—those few, stabilizing moments when I stay still enough in mind and body to touch base and establish connection with her for the rest of the day. I'd been working the Steps a long time, after all. Surely by now, "one day at a time" didn't have to mean *every* day one at a time, even when that day was looking stressful.

I made it across the mountain, got to the speech, listened, took notes, then hooked up my equipment and ran smack into an officious gatekeeper who declared that my man had no time for me. It's my job to be cheerfully assertive in such circumstances. I tried to insist, but got nowhere. Then I got angry. This is not to say I yelled and screamed and made a huge scene, but I did feel that old, familiar sock-in-the-stomach that anger used to give me, and I got testy. As a result, I spent the rest of that day and most of the next purging the bad chemicals loosed in my system by rampant bad feelings.

It was a sobering moment. It showed me how alive the old devilettes still were, hanging out inside me, just waiting for an opportunity to stage a coup. The important point wasn't what had happened to me—that I'd lost a not-very-important interview—but how I'd responded to the situation. I'd back-slud. I had not connected with Alice that morning, so I was unprotected from my own character defect. My defect had then gleefully seized on the Incident with the Officious Gatekeeper and roared back to life.

I really mean what I say here: *Any change for the better in my behavior will never be final.* My character defects will never be eliminated, and by myself, without Alice, I remain pretty defenseless against them. I don't think I'm quite as defenseless as I used to be, because I do have fairly entrenched habits of behaving decently. If I blew off Alice entirely, it would proba-bly take at least a couple of weeks for me to return fully to my old ways. But I *would* go back, just the way I'd backslud in the Incident of the Officious Gatekeeper. There will *always* be officious gatekeepers in life. The question is, how will I respond to them?

I see my ability to behave myself and be at peace as a gift that I must remember to ask for at the start of every day. If I don't take the time to connect every morning with that still, small pocket of Alice inside me, then I lose a small part of her strength and provide an opening for my lurking character defects. In other words, one day at a time means just that: one day at a time.

The Devil's in the Details (or Not)

I've discovered that Alice's calming presence is usually felt or lost in the small events of my day. Now please don't think I spend every waking hour monitoring myself. On the contrary, I probably spend less time thinking about myself nowadays than I have ever done before. I have my morning conversation with Alice, and then I let go of the controls and start enjoying the day. As long as I have established that conscious contact with the God of my understanding, I've turned on a gut-level monitoring system that warns me whenever I start heading toward screwy thinking. An alarm goes off just in time for me to veer away from the inevitable consequence of that screwy thinking, which is screwy behavior. I'm able to recognize that I have a clear choice *before* it is too late.

Let me emphasize that there is no magic wand involved here. My days run smoothly only as long as I take good care of myself and invite Alice to tag along. She and I function as allies in my life, not master and slave.

"Fearless" Pops up Again

Step Ten strongly suggests that I work diligently to develop and maintain habits of personal honesty to use in dealing with whatever I have to deal with. On my own, I would still spin the past, present and future, particularly when it came to presenting myself to myself. My ability to be straightforward at any given moment—to look at myself naked in the mirror, so to speak—appears to be as strong as my day's connection with Alice.

The word "fearlessly" does not appear in the traditional wording of Step Ten, but since I always added it in my heart, I've added it here. I know that by encouraging fearlessness I'm going against the cultural grain here, for fear has never been more popular. After all, the world is full of bad people doing bad things. We're put on Orange Alert over Christmas and Ramadan, for Pete's sake, because the Department of Homeland Security (doesn't that sound like something dreamed up by George Orwell) says more people are after us then than usual. Our government warns us to be extra careful as we go about our daily lives. Fear has become a cultural phenomenon, a subject for water cooler discussions, and a sales tool. The message that is pounded us is that it's prudent to organize our lives around our fears.

Phooey, I say.

The longer I hang out with Alice, the more firmly I believe in the existence of her polar opposite, the devil. Shall we call the old boy Mr. Lucifer? Mind you, I don't think of him as an entity that's lurking in the burning basement of the cosmos, but as a force actively at work in my heart and mind. I think of Mr. Lucifer as whatever tugs at me to return to my old dysfunctional ways, and I firmly believe that fear is Mr. Lucifer's manipulative tool of choice.

Let me be clear: Fear is not the same as common sense. I'm not advocating doing anything stupid or reckless in the name of proving one's fearlessness. Of course, there really are bad people doing terrible things. I've dealt with such people. For example, I fended off two rape attempts—one anonymous assault in the dark and one in my own kitchen from a seemingly respectable date. Believe me, I was afraid in both instances, particularly the second, because the assault came from inside what I wanted to believe was my own safety zone.

But that attempted date rape was also a liberating experience for me. After it happened, I had two choices: I could reason that I should be afraid of all apparently respectable men, or I could assume that creep was an anomaly and keep right on keeping on. Since I'm happily partnered with Charlie, you may assume I chose the latter.

That attempted date rape helped me understand something that I need to revisit constantly in order to avoid falling into Mr. Lucifer's clutches: There is simply no such thing as complete safety. No matter how defensively I live, bad things are sometimes going to happen to me, my loved ones, my country, and my world. I cannot imagine a more difficult climate for God to take root in than a society or life organized around the myth of safety. Its rock is fear, and its teachings—exclusion, condemnation, and oversimplification—are limiting beyond measure.

My Maternal Phobia

I'm not particularly afraid of the world or other people, but I did have a long-standing habit of fearing the disorderly contents of my own head and heart—most of the disorder having been generated by my decidedly high-strung mother. I used to put a tremendous amount of energy into keeping my emotional and physical distance from that woman. Her ability to mess with my head scared the living daylights out of me. Arguably, the biggest challenge of my adult life was my mother's decision, in her eighties, to relocate within ten miles of me.

I owe this woman my love and understanding of language, whatever social graces I have, a lot of my sense of humor, and almost every hour I've spent in therapist offices—whether from my inherited tendency to depression or the scary chaos of my childhood. Mother was smart, charming, a much respected teacher, quite beautiful, and crazy as a loon whenever intimacy loomed. There was an enormous disconnect between the at-home Mom and the at-large Mom. I have heard over and over again from others how sweet she was, which is one word I would *never* use to describe my mother.

There's really no other accurate way to phrase it: My mother's intense screwiness scared the daylights out of me. My relationship with her as a child had been so distorted by her frantic need to control, her periodic flights from reality, her fiendish tongue and temper, and, most of all, by her absolute dictum that we "not wash our family's dirty linen in public." This meant I was on my own in dealing with her periodically deranged and very scary behavior. Even after I'd escaped from her house, I could *feel* Mother sitting around in my head like a big spider, waiting to throw silk ropes over me so that she could reel me back into her crazed control. If you, too, had a problematical childhood, I'm sure you understand how I felt. If you didn't, just imagine Dr. Jekyll/Mr. Hyde as your mother instead of the one you had.

My elderly mother landed on my turf because my big sister had been urging her to relocate close to *her*. My father had died, and Mother was living alone in the distant retirement community where she and Dad had settled years ago. The final, complicating factor in her staying there came when Mom voluntarily stopped driving after a small accident. At that point, my sister became concerned about how she could continue to manage life independently. My sister, who is far more together, organized, and dutiful than I, was prepared to intervene actively in Mother's life.

I was not. My main concern when it came to Mother was maintaining the emotional détente I had reached with my childhood. I was scared of returning to its emotional chaos and rock-solid certain my mental health could only be maintained by doing what I could for Mom from a concerned distance. Besides, I reasoned, Mother was nothing if not resourceful. When she'd stopped driving, she'd found and hired a driver who danced around her like a suitor—and told me many times what a sweet lady my mother was.

A few months passed. My sister found an independent-living facility very close to her and 600 miles from me. In between my sister's frequent business trips around the country and the world, she urged Mom to pack up and move there. Mom, increasingly crippled by arthritis, finally admitted that it would be nice to live close to one of her daughters. I thought this a fine idea and graciously announced I'd be happy to fly out to visit her in her new home close to my sister. Mother agreed to move.

Then, one fateful Saturday afternoon, the phone rang. It was Mom, and she sounded distressed. She really *did* want to live close to one of her daughters, she said, but she was worried about moving close to my sister because she was so often out of town. Mom was worried she'd move to a strange place where she didn't know anyone except a constantly traveling daughter.

I remember that moment as an out-of-body experience. The therapized, sane me withdrew myself from the conversation and became an observer, while this lunatic inside me took over and said, "Well, Mother, why don't you come and live closer to me?"

She agreed immediately.

I hung up the phone and felt rage, which I was sane enough to recognize as terror or post-traumatic stress. My life had been so simple and happy for the last decade. It had taken years of work—first therapy, then sobriety, then Twelve Stepping and conversations with Alice to leave behind the la-la land where I'd been born and raised. I'd had these few years of blessed, peaceful real life, and now—just like that—I'd gone insane and invited the Darth Vader of my psyche to breach the buffer zone I'd constructed between us. My mother—the person who'd wreaked active havoc in my childhood and residual havoc in my adult years—would soon be close enough to inflict yet more havoc in my late middle-age. How was I ever going to survive daily contact with her, without emotionally returning to Mordor and the slopes of Mount Doom? I was *really* terrified.

Well, what a needless tempest in a teapot that was. I took several deep breaths (actually many deep breaths), used the Steps, conversed with Alice, talked with—and listened to—other people. I gave up being terrified of what had happened in the past and what might happen in the future. This allowed me to stop trying to *control* what would happen in the future, and sanely prepare for the Maternal Invasion.

When Mother came, I faked a warm welcome and settled her into her new apartment in a high-rise for the elderly. I lectured myself six ways from Sunday about staying in the present, dealing with what was actually going on with this lady, and not viewing Mother through yesterday's very dark glasses. A few weeks passed, and I began to realize that the woman living close to me was pretty harmless, just a frail old lady who was delighted to be living in her very own space for the first time in her life. It gradually dawned on me that my mother was not really interested in doing anything other than exploring life as a person who didn't have to get along with anyone else at close quarters.

In other words, I got busy and forced myself to be brave enough to stay in the present. I worked Step Ten like a woman on a mission. Which I guess I was—the mission being my own continued peace of mind. Every night I'd take an objective inventory of what had actually happened that day and *only* what had happened that day—doing my best to be fearless and thorough. Thanks to this self-imposed discipline, the crazy woman of my childhood remained in the past where she belonged, and I cautiously began to experience my mother as other people saw her—witty, extremely well-educated, and charming.

Mother and Charlie became chums. The three of us had a lot of sedate good times together. When Mom became ill, I *wanted* to take care of her, which I take as hard evidence of the Miraculous Healing of Martha. Mom and I were given the gift of a nice couple of years. By the time of her death, I'd begun to feel compassion for this woman who'd been so happy finally living on her own, and who'd had such sanity-shattering difficulty being part of a family. I'll take compassion over rage or fear every time as a feeling to lug around inside my head and heart.

So looking back at the Invasion of Mom, I can say that

everything worked out fine. To explain why, I have to use a lot of Twelve-Step truisms: I *fearlessly* got out of my own way, relied on the God of my understanding, and *let* things work out fine.

Dear me. To this day, whenever I write or speak a sophistry-ridden sentence such as the last one, I cringe. But I've also learned humility over my years of Twelve Stepping. If it works, don't worry about how it sounds when you talk about it.

Taking Our Best Shot at Complete Honesty

I burble on about fear because, in my experience, fear and dishonesty are inexorably linked. By fear, I mean any sort of generalized sense of dread or alarm that limits our ability to face what is really going on in our lives, our worlds and ourselves today. To work the Steps effectively, you and I must face ourselves and our worlds exactly as they are right now—good times, warts, dangers, complications, and all.

We're still going to screw up sometimes. That's a given. The important thing, as far as Step Ten goes, is to be *fearless* about recognizing these screwups as soon as possible. If we don't, we'll soon substitute dishonest explanations, justifications, and excuses for our behavior, and these will corrode our hearts and minds.

Honesty requires consistent but uncomplicated maintenance of fearlessness. We're brave when we can freely admit our mistakes. We're arrogant or cowardly when we don't. There are no excuses, *ever*, for lying to ourselves. And the punishment for such arrogance and cowardliness for me has always been a feeling of distance from Alice and from any

Alice-given peace of mind. I've found courage is best practiced as a habit. In my own experience, it begins by fearlessly facing the daily details of my behavior and thoughts.

Onward!

Think about how good it feels to stretch your body and then give stretching your heart and mind a shot. All you've got to do is regularly, diligently, and *fearlessly* work Step Ten. Don't borrow trouble and don't let yourself lapse into the melodrama of inventing fearful scenarios of what might happen. Instead, develop a habit of staying in the real present, checking in regularly with the God of your understanding, and paying attention to your conscience. When you realize you're on the wrong track, stop! Make amends if you need to, shift gears, and get on with your day.

Make it a ritual to revisit your day at the end of it. Check in with God and, together, take an honest look at how you did. If you screwed up, face it in God's company, learn from it, plan to make whatever amends are called for as soon as possible, and sleep well.

THE KICK START

- Step Ten is like working out. You always have a choice about doing it or not doing it. While there will always be good *excuses* for not doing it, there are no good *reasons*. If you lead a sedentary life, the results are guaranteed: Too much weight and too little energy. If you blow off Step Ten, you'll quickly become muddle-headed and lose the clarity you worked so hard to achieve in the first nine Steps.

- Don't make Step Ten too complicated or too serious. The goal here is to develop the ability to look at yourself and your life simply, directly and honestly.

- Use any kind of check-in system that works. I know folks who start each day with formal prayers and a written gratitude list, who scrupulously journal their transgressions, and have long conversations with other folks to sort out the details of their days. Then there's me. I say good morning to Alice, hang out with her during the day, and make it a habit to actively enjoy and be grateful for every day that's a good day. I also make it a habit to listen hard to my conscience because it always lets me know when I'm feeding myself a bunch of baloney. I try to be quick to apologize for my trespasses, and thanks to one of Alice's small miracles, am usually quick to forgive those who trespass against me.

- Step Ten is basically a good habit, and, like any habit, it becomes second nature when you do it long enough. Having good habits instead of screwy ones is a great reward of working the Steps.

11

A Direct Line to Alice

STEP ELEVEN

**I WILL DEVELOP THE HABIT OF
STAYING IN CLOSE TOUCH WITH
THE GOD OF MY UNDERSTANDING.**

Before I got sober, I remember being stalled at a red light in a long line of heavy traffic. The car ahead of me was an old station wagon, filled with kids and covered with bumper-stickers. I had nothing to do but seethe and read the stickers: *Wall Drugs, Peace is the Way, I Have No Idea Where I'm Going, Elvis for President*, and, of course, *Today is the First Day of the Rest of Your Life.* I remember staring at that last one, the clarion call of the chipper, and wanting desperately to stick my thumbs in my ears, wiggle my fingers, stick out my tongue, and shriek, "BLAAAAHH!"

Well, my, my! How time and the Twelve Steps can change a person. I am now willing to state with happy conviction that today really *is* the first day of the rest of my life, and, as such, I plan to enjoy the hell out of it. I'm confident I have an excellent shot at feeling good about the twenty-four hours ahead of me—maybe even accomplishing something worthwhile and satisfying over the course of it, and having fun while doing it. I don't expect to be spending a lot of energy trying not to screw up and then feeling badly when I do. I'll most likely shy away from stress, except the stress that's inherent in my job. I'll keep my senses of humor and proportion active enough to remember that all I can do is my best, and it's not the end of the world if I make a mistake. I have a good possibility of going to bed tonight at peace with myself and everyone else.

About Fun

By this point in working the Steps, your definition of "fun" may have changed. I know mine has. I used to think that for something to be fun, it had to feel hard-driven and jazzed. Having fun meant my emotions became supercharged. La-La land also figured prominently in my perception of fun, for when I was looking forward to doing something, I would spend energy picturing how it would be, then I would gauge how much fun I was having by how close the actual doing of it came to those pictures. I worked hard in those days at getting "fun" right. Having a good time in those days was very labor intensive.

I once interviewed the late great bluesman, John Jackson. During the interview, I kept asking Mr. Jackson to define the blues. He kept answering by telling me another story about how his life had worked into his music. Back home, listening to the tape, I finally got it. Blues and life were synonymous to

John Jackson; the former was the musical embodiment of the latter.

It's pretty much the same thing for me now when it comes to my definition of fun. *Fun = living.* I'm having fun most of the time, for having fun has morphed into a simple habit of being—one in which I feel relaxed, focused, and square with God, other people and myself. These days, I have fun doing everything from dancing the night away to vacuuming. (Actually, the claim that I find vacuuming fun might be stretching things a bit. I probably still hate vacuuming most of the time.) I've found that the amount of fun I have these days is directly proportionate to the strength and clarity of my connection with Alice.

Phoning Home

My Dad traveled a lot when I was growing up. He hated most of those trips—hated being away from home, hated all the impersonal food, hated the anonymous hotel rooms and the superficial conversations. The one exception to his hatred of business travel was when he went to San Francisco. Dad loved San Francisco—its people, its food, and its fanciful buildings perched alongside impossibly pitched streets. I think Dad would have moved all of us out to San Francisco if he could have. He was a city person at heart, his tastes locked in place during his formative years at Columbia University in New York City.

Whenever Dad was in San Francisco and had time between business appointments, he'd prowl the city—not so much the high-end destinations or the traditional tourist stops, as the city's ethnic underbelly. He would come home with funny presents for all of us, like the little Chinese "robin," brightly colored as a parrot, that we placed on the wooden window valance of our back den so it could keep its beady, unblinking eye on us. My mother gleefully referred to this ridiculous "robin" as Big Brother.

Dad also came home from San Francisco with tales of multi-cultural adventures. He'd tell them to my mother, sister, and me immediately, and then tell them again to guests who came trooping through our house for cocktails or dinner. There was the one about a panhandler who'd asked him for a dollar. Dad didn't have a dollar and so impulsively had given the panhandler a five. The panhandler then proceeded to give Dad change, saying that he'd asked for a dollar, and that was all he could take in good conscience. Dad walked away, only to feel a tap on his shoulder. It was the panhandler asking for his change back.

And there was the one about the tombstone.

It had marked a child's grave in some Christian sect's churchyard. There was a plastic telephone on top of the tombstone, and the inscription on the stone read, "direct line to Jesus." This had tickled my father no end. I think he enjoyed the simplicity of the family's faith even though he could never have shared it. Dad said he'd picked up the receiver, listened, and there'd been no one on the other end—but then my dad was an insistent atheist.

I am not. I'm not a member of any sect, either—Jewish, Manichaean, Christian, Buddhist, Hindu, Zoroastrian. And I don't yet keep a plastic phone on my bedside table to call the good Lord. But I am a believer in God, in my fast friend and companion, whom I choose to consider as the ever-approachable Alice. I came to belief slowly and ungracefully, traveling to it along the bumpy road of my own mistakes. All I brought along on the journey was a desire to live a satisfying life, a willingness to learn to look out at the world and see it as it really is, a curiosity about facing the way things actually work. I've come to accept the dependability of a single, simple habit of being that I formed through working the first ten Steps: I accept that my partnership with Alice is the foundation of everything that goes right in my life.

Again, I'm not talking about the things that happen to me, but about how I experience and respond to those things. And I do believe myself to be lucky, in the greater view of life, to have been a substance abuser. I have the convenience of a few clear-cut disasters in my memory to remind me of how screwed up my life was when I ran the zoo (apologies, again, to Dr. Seuss). Plus, substance abuse led me to the Twelve Steps, which I've found to be a way to bring order and a sense of quiet satisfaction to a life that for years was lived at a messy, full-tilt, unsatisfying boogie.

So Where Are We?

We appear to be poised one Step away from the end of working the Steps. This means we've hooked up with the God of our understanding, with whose help we've physically, intellectually, and spiritually confronted ourselves naked in the mirror. We've dealt fearlessly and forthrightly—to the best of our current ability—with both our character defects and our checkered pasts. And we've become much better able to manage our character defects and put the past behind us.

Where we're *not*, however, is nose-to-nose with perfection.

We still make mistakes, we still have screwy thoughts, we're still haunted by impulses to do stupid things that we still tell ourselves we should not want to do. In other words, you and I are still human. But despite those remaining less-than-stellar attributes, if your experience of working the Steps so far has been at all like mine, you are beginning to have a new sense of peace and joy in your head and in your heart. You are also beginning to feel real hope about yourself and your future. Inside you now is a truly satisfying knowledge that you have, indeed, changed for the better. You're more honest, calmer, kinder, less defensive, and less burdened with emotional baggage. Let's face it: You are much less of a screwup and you have every reason to hope that further such changes for the better are in your future.

For me, there was a growing confidence that, as long as I maintained my relationship with Alice, I would be all right no matter what happened to me. And, I'm happy to add, the last decade or so has proved this to be true. Certainly, I've been through some difficult stuff, but difficult stuff has lost its ability to create feelings of despair, hopelessness, self-pity, or lasting anger. I haven't needed to act out destructively. I've certainly flirted with the impulse to act out, but so far I've always been able to pull back from doing anything really self-destructive. I'm happy to report I've been a pretty contented camper for quite a while now.

So what *does* arriving at Step Eleven mean, if it doesn't mean approaching perfection?

Step Eleven found me poised to go nose-to-nose with the Serenity Prayer: *God, grant me the serenity to accept the things I cannot change, the courage to change the things I can, and the wisdom to know the difference.* As a supplication this prayer is so deceptively direct and uncomplicated in its wording that its profundity, as well as its call for emotional self-discipline, can slide right by us.

Whenever I say this simple prayer, which is often, I feel I'm asking Alice to keep me grounded in what's real. The Serenity Prayer's simply worded request for equilibrium seems to demand more of me every time I use it. Over time, I've come to accept that whatever serenity I've gotten has come hand-in-hand with an ever-deepening acceptance that, if there's any changing to be done, I'm the only one I can expect to do it. It's pretty clear to me—as I hope it is now clear to you—that if I'm to have any peace of mind, I must accept others exactly as they are and relate to them accordingly. I blush to think of the energy I've used educating other people on how they should think or feel, and then taking on the responsibility of changing them. Who did I think I was? Alice? Pul-*leeze!* Certainly I've seen people change, but the impetus for such change has always come from them.

Living, Not Working

Here and now, as we are poised to tackle Step Eleven, it's important to accept down to our toes that *the Steps are not a cure for anything; instead they are a thinking and living process.* I've really misspoken when I've referred to *working* the Steps. What I'm really encouraging myself and you to do is to form the habit of *living* the Steps. I've used "working" because we Americans have a well-documented cultural tendency to crave action. We like tasks and lists of projects that come with specific instructions so we can check them off our to-do list and feel like we're getting somewhere. So until now, I've mostly stuck with "working" as a way to talk about what you and I are up to. But we've now arrived at Step Eleven, which I found to be the gateway Step to a changed attitude toward living. To me, it only makes sense to talk more accurately about what we're actually doing.

Certainly, I *did* things while wading through the Steps. I made various lists and went through periods where I deliberately opened up my internal cans of worms and took a good, long look inside them. With the wisdom of hindsight, what I think I was really doing with all this activity was actually learning to live my life close to the God of my understanding.

As an example of what I mean by this, let me zoom back to my former career as a queen of small market television. Years ago, I hosted a TV talk show, so for two seasons I was a tatty sort of media queen-ette. It was a mind-boggling experience. Everybody in town who didn't have a nine-to-five job seemed to feel they knew me intimately, and why not? I was in their living room every morning from nine until nine-thirty. Complete strangers came up to me in the grocery store, invariably to tell me what they thought about my hair or my clothes. It was as close to being a celebrity as I ever care to come. My daughter hated it. She and I could never go anywhere without someone else demanding her mother's attention.

Before my talk show stint, I was running a small, scratch-cooking restaurant in partnership with my then-husband, and I only applied for the talk show job in the first place because that man said I couldn't get the job! I'd not had one moment of prior broadcasting experience before I was hired, unless you count reading the morning announcements over the public address system in junior high school.

The TV station had auditioned lots of other people for the job, yet they hired me. Why? Because I had the rare ability to be completely comfortable while looking straight into the black hole of a camera. I instinctively knew that black hole led to other people who were part of whatever conversation I was having during the show, even though I couldn't see them. It's not much of a talent to write home about, but it is useful in broadcasting. I feel the same way these days when I'm speaking into a microphone in the on-air studio at the radio station. I know in my gut that I'm talking directly to someone I can't see.

That is exactly how I've come to feel about Alice through working and living the Steps. I cannot see or hear her, but I know she's there. And I know I can connect directly with her anytime I wish—without a plastic telephone or a TV camera or a microphone. All I have to do is be quiet inside, and she is there. With her presence comes a great fund of quiet strength, of good humor, of patience, of even-temperedness, and generosity of heart. With her presence comes the serenity to accept the things I cannot change, the courage to change the things I can, and the wisdom to know the difference. I include Alice in my life these days as instinctively as I used to include the people beyond the camera lens's black hole. I just know she's there.

If you are not religious, it's a lot to swallow, I know. Faith in God is not a decision that can ever be reached intellectually—approached, maybe, but never fully reached. There are no measurable facts to prove such a presence in our lives. My father would have thought this whole book the worst kind of sentimental sophistry, and so may you.

If you *are* religious, it may be a lot to swallow as well. Religion relies on ritual and writings—as explained and interpreted by leaders. The Steps ask you to listen to your God as she/he/it speaks through your own conscience. In working the Twelve Steps, espousing the tenants of any one faith is of less importance than your own kind and moral actions.

For me, connection with Alice has become a way of life. All I can offer you is my own experience as encouragement to make a similar leap of faith. I leapt through working the Steps. I worked the Steps because I was out of other options. What I hope is that this book will encourage you to work the Steps in your own way, in your own time, and hopefully before things have come to such a pass that you have no other choice. I hope you will use whatever's bothering you—whatever it is that made you pick up this book in the first place—as impetus to continue plugging away at the Twelve Steps.

So What Are We Supposed to Do?

What exactly does developing "the habit of staying in close touch with the God of my understanding" mean anyway?

Again, all I have to offer is my own bumpy experience. I'm a fiercely independent cuss. I will never be especially receptive to specific suggestions from others about how I should run my life. It took me years to build time with Alice into my day and to give these moments of connection the same disciplined approach I give to working out and brushing my teeth. But the years passed, Alice was patient, I allowed myself to change, and now I don't just spend regular time with her out of habit, I do it with joy and gratitude.

Just like the Quaker lady I talked about in the chapter on Step Two, I now think of my time with Alice as dessert. I check in whenever my head or my heart needs a rest, sometimes from busy-ness, sometimes from stress, sometimes just because I'm happy.

My morning and evening check-ins have become pretty firm daily rituals. I try to begin these with gratitude, for one great gift of the Steps for me is the ability to *feel* my blessings. The check-in process for me is informal. I take a moment to feel really happy about whatever in my life is going well.

Then I move on to the less-than-successful areas of my life. There's another Twelve Step prayer that's a simple request: *Please give me knowledge of your will for me today and the strength to carry it out.* I'm a long way from being able to ask for only that. I still need a lot of specific help, so what I usually do is check in about the specific things going on that could conceivably overwhelm, hurt, confuse, or annoy me. I ask that I be able to approach them fearlessly and with a clear head and open heart. The good news is that, after years of working the Steps, there are many more blessing than screwups to chat about. Step Eleven is challenging in its simplicity. All it requires is the formation of habits of fearless personal honesty and faith, which were once as foreign to me as flying.

Doing Our Part

I want to emphasize that it will always be my responsibility to take the best care of myself I can in all the obvious ways—to actually do the things I know are good for me, and steer clear of things that I know will make me feel addled and bad. I need to eat right, exercise, get enough sleep, and stay away from situations that will pointlessly agitate me.

In my times of prayer, I may ask God for enough self-discipline so that I can do what I need to do in order to feel good, *but it is still up to me to do these things.* I cannot repeat that often enough. My relationship with Alice is a partnership. I am not her puppet. This partnership comes with responsibilities that I ignore at my own peril.

Sometimes what I can only describe as pure cussedness—the stirrings of those tenacious little devilettes inside me—rises up. But the Steps have given me mechanisms for sorting out my cussedness and minimizing the effect those devilettes have on my life. Turning to Alice through Step Eleven is my best defense against my own stupidity.

THE KICK START

- Step Eleven is essentially about turning Step Ten into a habit of being. The key is to be diligent about paying attention to whatever you call that inner voice (your conscience?) that sounds off when your character defects are again threatening a take-over.

- Whenever that inner voice sounds an alarm, stop whatever you're doing and listen to what that inner voice has to say! Believe me, whatever you're doing is less important than stopping it at that moment.

- Listen to that inner voice. If it tells you that one of your character defects has roared back into life and seized control of your actions or thoughts, do whatever it takes to tone down the level of this control. Visit with God, say and mean the Serenity Prayer.

- If you absolutely cannot stop what you are doing, ask God for help in doing the next right thing, and keep in mind one of the principal precepts taught to all medical students: *primum non nocere*, first do no harm.

- Develop the habit of allowing the God of your understanding to take a prominent part in your inner conversation throughout the day. If you're a formal person, you can use times of formal prayer to do this. If you're as casual as I am, just keep the lines of communication open and develop a habit of both chatting with and listening to God.

● Don't worry, don't judge yourself or others, and don't be fearful. Let go of the controls, and have faith in the God of your understanding. Do the best you can with God's help, and let yourself enjoy your day. Over time, if you are diligent in your living of the Steps, you'll look back and see how your days have gotten better and better.

12

The Place Just Right

STEP TWELVE

I WILL COMMIT MYSELF TO PRACTICE THESE PRINCIPLES IN EVERYTHING I DO.

'Tis a gift to be simple, 'tis a gift to be free.

'Tis a gift to come down where you want to be.

And when you find yourself in a place just right

You will be in the valley of love and delight.

—old Shaker hymn

This story is from my radio freelancing days, before I met Alice and began working the Twelve Steps.

I picked up a hitchhiker on Route 522, just south of Flint Hill, Virginia, close to where it crosses the Jordan River. It was mid-December and snowing heavily. I was out on the road looking for Christmas stories and instead came upon a man walking down this back country road with his thumb out. He had on a light coat and carried no luggage, so I thought he was a motorist in trouble. There were no other cars in sight. The wind was blowing, the snow was piling up fast, and the cold was biting. Even as a heathen, I believed I was my brother's keeper, so—against all conventional wisdom—I pulled over.

The man came running through the snow and climbed into the cab of my pickup, smiling broadly. He had a lot of teeth; almost all of them were bad. "Howdy ma'am," he said. "I want to thank you for stopping."

"Glad to do it," I said, trying not to dwell on those teeth.

We took off down the snowy road. My passenger immediately began to talk politics, rocking back and forth in his seat and banging his knee rhythmically with a fist. He wandered freely among parties and philosophies. The more he talked, the more agitated he got, as though someone were disagreeing with him. I had not said a word.

"Did you run your car off the road?" I asked, trying to get him off politics.

"No, ma'am," he said. "I'm not out here because I'm in trouble. I'm just out here."

I did not ask out here from where. This guy was crazy. We drove on. He went back to his rocking, his banging, his politics. I went back to silence.

Abruptly the man sat still. "How far you going?" he asked.

"How far are *you* going?" I countered.

"Oh, I'm just going," he said.

Whoa, I thought. "I can take you another few miles," I said.

"Okay," he said.

I felt his hand putting pressure on the seat close to my right thigh. I didn't look at him, but I could feel him grinning. "I'll have to let you out soon," I said.

"That's okay." He sounded quite happy.

"Let you out in the snow, I mean."

"Okay."

We drove in silence for a mile or so. The snow continued to pour down. The man's fingers crept closer. They were now touching the seam of my jeans.

"You weren't going to pick me up, were you?" he said.

"I beg your pardon?" Now I didn't dare to look at him. I was scared, and I knew that when you're dealing with crazy people who could be prone to violence, looking scared is not a good idea.

"Back there. You drove by and you weren't going to pick me up, were you?" he said, brightly, happily.

I didn't say anything.

The man went on in the same bright, happy voice. "You weren't going to pick me up because you thought I might hurt you. Ain't that the truth?"

I concentrated on the twin tunnels my headlights made in the snow. There was a country store up ahead that would most likely be open. I could let this lunatic out there and we'd both be safe. If he tried anything before we got to the safety of that store, I would backhand him across the throat with my right hand and try to keep control of the wheel with my left.

Suddenly the man leaned forward and patted my knee. "You weren't going to pick me up because you thought I was going to hurt you," he said. Another pat, but then his hand moved away. "Don't you worry, pretty lady," he said, sounding like a happy child. "I'm not going to hurt you. I'm not going to hurt you *now*. You see, I've found the Lord."

Hallelujah!

I've never forgotten that guy. Here's to him, wherever he is. And here's to you and I, as well, for there's real joy for us and everyone we touch, once we're able to plant our feet on a path that keeps us doing the right thing and rids us of our compulsion to screw up. However that hitchhiker found the strength to do the right thing that snowy day, I'm happy for both of us that he did.

I found my version of that strength years later by working the first eleven Steps. But now here we are, discovering that that the price of *keeping* that joy bright and alive in us is practicing certain principles in everything we do.

"What principles are those?" you ask. "Might we be a tad more specific?"

Yes and no. I'm firmly convinced that my old pals, the devilettes, immediately start sharpening their claws whenever they hear me set myself up as a person who—because I've worked the Steps, doesn't use my drugs of choice anymore and doesn't constantly lose my temper—is now qualified to tell others how they should run their lives

So the best I can offer is my take on what the principles of Step Twelve are *not*. I think they are not a bunch of rigid behavioral rules that, if you follow them, will make you into an official Good Person. In fact, I imagine the head good ol' boy himself, Mr. Lucifer, dances a jig whenever *any* of us adopts a strict rule by which we feel empowered to judge other people's decisions, behaviors, and lifestyles. Think about it—once we're busy disapproving, judging, gossiping, or trying to control other people's behavior, we're distracted from hearing anything useful God might have to say.

I speak about this with the sad authority of experience. I used to be quite an expert on how other people should run their lives. That was, of course, before I worked the Steps and took responsibility for running my own.

As I've said before, there are no rules about living the Steps, only guidelines to help us put forth our best efforts made in God's company. As far as this program goes, what we actually do with our day, how we do it, and whom we do it with are all left up to us. The only specific ongoing instructions we get are Steps Ten and Eleven: We're supposed to admit it when we goof up and make amends as soon as possible, and we're supposed to check in frequently during the day with the God of our understanding and pay attention to what we hear.

As for Step Twelve, I've concluded it's nothing but a vigorous reminder that the Steps are *not* a set of regulations, but are instead a *thinking and living process built around honesty.* Step Twelve means that in order to keep the good we got out of working Steps One through Eleven, we must wrap our hearts and minds around the habit of being that we established while working them, and carry that habit of being onward through everything we do.

Our Part in the Partnership

You started reading this book because your life feels screwed up. You've been screwing up—doing things you didn't want to do simply because you didn't feel square enough in your own skin not to do them. Since you've read this far, I can assume that you're open to the possibility that you, too, have a chance to stop screwing up by working the Twelve Steps. You've probably realized that it's an equal-opportunity chance—open for all of us to take—but that it does come with requirements that cannot be fudged. To have a shot at what the Steps have to offer, you have to be honest, and you have to be willing to give up the idea that your own brain is God. Even if the only higher power you acknowledge is your conscience, *you must include some higher power in your life to work the Steps.*

Now your road to the Steps was probably different from mine, but I'm willing to wager serious amounts of chocolate that our motives and experiences along the way were essentially the same. Both of us gave the Steps a try in the first place because we felt bad, and both of us were after a way to learn from and leave behind the mistakes of the past.

While working the Steps, we both uncovered our hunger for an ingrained faith in a God of our understanding who could bring us peace, and let us get on with a well-lived life. I hooked up with Alice; you hooked up with Jack or Sophia or Zeus, or Whomever. The Steps do not pretend to be an authority on God's proper name.

The Steps also make no attempt to *explain* how God works in either of us, where God lives, what God has to do with our life stories, what God does on her own time, what God thinks of you or me or our siblings or our colleagues at work. All I know for certain about God is that she will remain forever something you and I are not. I'm also pretty certain that the moment you or I start theorizing about how or why she does her thing is the moment we diminish her to human size and limit her understanding to the scope of our own.

I sometimes find it very difficult to pay attention to God. I live surrounded by noise, and Alice is *sooooo* soft spoken. It's up to me to provide enough quiet time in my life and quiet space in my head to hear what Alice has to say.

The longer I hang out with Alice, the more confident I am that I can get help from her in dealing with any of my persistent and pesky dysfunctional urges. But it's my job to recognize those urges and ask for that help without either melodrama or justification. If I lie to myself or Alice about my own motives or desires—on any level, for any reason—it makes nonsense out of my prayers. And soon it will once again make nonsense out of my life.

My Own Step-Twelve Principles

Over the years, I've boiled Step Twelve down to simply trying to do the next, right thing. However, my days frequently seem as confusing and complicated as an NFL defensive scheme, and there is an alarming number of times during any given twenty-four-hour period when it's not clear to me what the next right thing to do is. When this pickle arises, I've found things go pretty well as long as I stop and speak to Alice, pay close attention to what she says, take my best shot at doing the next right thing, and remain ready to reevaluate my actions or opinions once all the dust has settled.

Here are my personal guidelines:

- I try to be kind, thoughtful, and completely honest with myself and as honest with others as kindness allows. This is an ever-evolving process.

- I try to approach people who are different from me, or who don't behave as I think they should, with curiosity and compassion, and without judgment. I don't have to *like* anybody, but I do have to *accept* everyone as they are. This is still a huge struggle for me. I am so opinionated!

- I try very, very hard not to attempt control of other people or events.

- I try to exercise self-control, not in a rigid, teeth-gritting sense, but in the sense of reminding myself that it's stupid to do things I know are stupid.

A Final Look Back

I came to the Twelve Steps as a mess—addicted not only to drugs and alcohol, but to self-spin, arrogance, being judgmental, temper tantrums, and a few other equally unpleasant behaviors. Steps One, Two, and Three effectively lowered the volume level in my head so I could form a connection with Alice. Steps Four through Nine cleared away the mountain of emotional rubble I'd built up in my head and heart that had blocked my access to Alice's comfort and company. Taken together, the first nine Steps introduced me to Alice, as well as suggesting practices to follow that, with her ready assistance, could jettison all the past sadness, anger, guilt right out of my psyche.

Steps Ten, Eleven, and Twelve were where I was headed, however. These are the Steps that will make this day a good day when I practice them. Step Ten keeps me from accumulating a new stockpile of debilitating emotions and so keeps my mountain of grief and anger from rebuilding. Step Eleven reminds me I must communicate openly with Alice in order to be honest, kind, and productive. Step Twelve tells me to do the next right thing—judged *only* by Alice speaking through the dictates of my conscience.

I've also come to realize now that true humility is healthy. For me, emotions such as self-satisfaction, triumph, self-importance, and arrogance are addictive mind-sets I've got to shy away from because they weaken my relationship with Alice. I find such emotions as dangerous to my peace of mind as my drugs of choice.

Of course, I still find trying to be so bloody high-minded a real challenge to my self-image. It makes me feel like a full-fledged prig even to contemplate the thought of checking in constantly with God (even a God I've dubbed Alice) as a *modus operandi.* But I'm also convinced it's better to feel like a prig than to feel angry and sad, and to go about making myself and others miserable. I've found through years of practice, that Steps Ten, Eleven and Twelve are what allow me to live large. Through them, I gradually got so busy being happy that I no longer had the time, energy, or inclination to screw up nearly as much.

Here's Looking at You, Kid

So there they are, my Twelve Steps for dealing with general screwups—based on a time-tested method of recovery from my very human propensity to insist on going my own way down an unhappy path. Over time, if you keep plugging away at them, you will finally stop damaging yourself and others, making a fool of yourself, and generally screwing up. It takes time and effort, and God. But there are millions in recovery from drug and alcohol abuse, smoking, overeating, gambling, sexual addiction, all of whom are living testaments that this spiritual process works.

I do hope you'll try the Steps. The only thing you have to lose is the unhappiness that made you to pick up this book.

About Happiness

I once dated a man—a very smart, mega-educated professor—who shied away like a spooked horse from the question, "Are you happy?" Not "Are you happy with me?" But "Are you happy with life in general?" Instead of answering with a simple yes or no, he would talk about the nature of happiness, the philosophical construct of emotions, the unreliability of his own, ever-shifting viewpoint.

The guy had had lots of therapy. Nothing about the inside of his head and heart was *ever* simple. At the time, I listened and thought, he is *so* profound!

Now I think, what nonsensical sound and fury that was! For me, post-Stepping happiness is akin to love: I know it when I feel it, and when I feel it, I embrace it with all my heart and soul and might, and I'm unashamed to shout *"I feel good!"*—just like James Brown.

13

Let the Good Times Keep on Rolling!

Charlie and I were an artist colony romance. We were two midlife rock 'n' rollers delighted to bump into each other, yet sensible enough, for once in our lives, to marry. I was a year into the Twelve Steps, stuck on Step Two, resisting the oh-so-patient Alice with every over-intellectualized fiber of my being.

I was broke, but Charlie had saved a little money. We used it to buy land, eleven-and-a-half acres of woods, surrounded by hundreds and hundreds of acres of logging forest; home to pileated woodpeckers, bears, foxes, wild turkeys, and very few people. We bought our first trailer at a bank auction. It was ancient repo that came stuffed with a startling variety and number of harvest gold and avocado appliances. The bank let us have it for $750. We hauled it out to our land and moved into it with no water and no septic field. But the green refrigerator and the gold stove still worked, and so there we were—homeowners.

That first winter was a real adventure, like an extended stay at survival camp. There were a couple of genuine blizzards, which are rare in Virginia. We were without power for days at a time, carrying water down the snow-clogged logging road we used as a driveway. By the next winter, we'd saved enough to dig a well. By the next, we'd bought a newer trailer and put in a septic system. We called our second trailer the Palace because, for us, it was one. Like the Jeffersons, we were moving on up.

Amherst County soil is mostly a thin layer of clay over shale. Our land was on Buffalo Ridge, a running, rise of land named for the Buffalo hunted by its first inhabitants, the Monacan Indians. Mixed in with the shale on our land was a lot of big rocks. Gardening on our land was a challenge. You didn't grow flowers without first swinging a pick.

Charlie's first nickname for me was "Hoss," for workhorse, because of my stamina with garden tools. I'd go out to a spot I was determined to grow flowers and whack at the thin, stony soil for hours. I'd always loved gardening, but before I'd always worked it in around everything else I had going on. But now here I was, broke, married, not drinking or drugging, living in rural Amherst County. There was plenty of time for gardening, no money to do much else, and not much else to do anyway.

My gardens got bigger over the years as I tenaciously hacked at that rocky soil. Annuals and perennials alike bloomed mightily, and I would wander through them at the end of the day awash in delight and satisfaction.

I loved our trailers, too. I threw out all my preconceived notions of what my adult home should look like and simply nested where I was. I put everything pretty that Charlie and I owned out where we could see it. An ugly, enormous down sofa had come with the Palace, because it had been too heavy for the former owners to move out and it was too comfortable for us to get rid of. We'd covered it with one of Charlie's grandmother's quilts, which hid most of its aesthetic sins, and left it in the living room. I didn't have to look at it much when I was inside, because I'd usually sit on it and look at something else.

Most summer evenings Charlie and I stayed outside until dark, frolicking like a couple of kids who want to play just one more game of Red Rover. When darkness had come and the fireflies were out, we'd finally drag ourselves in and sit together on that sofa. Lamps would be on, so I could see through the kitchen into our bedroom, see the spines of my grandfather's books on the bookshelves, the gleam of family silver on the plastic paneled kitchen shelves, see the old rocker in the bedroom. I'd listen to the hum and thrum of the night-time woods through the open windows, and I'd realize I didn't feel the need to *do* anything. That was the first time in a long, long time, I could remember contentedly *being*—being in the same way I'd felt as a child in my grandparent's house.

Over those same years, I'd also kept plugging away at my acceptance of Alice. I knew I needed to argue less, listen more, and learn from my own experience while working the Steps. I needed to break through my compulsion to be the boss in favor of hooking up with Alice and doing our thing together. I still found it extremely hard to *do* less while living, which is what hooking up with Alice really amounts to. I also found it scary to trust in some entity I couldn't see or even pretend to understand. But the summers passed, the winters came and went, and I gradually recognized that I had a deep hunger to do just those things—as well as having a deep, deep hunch that they were healthy things for me to do. So, I kept at the Steps the way I kept after Amherst county dirt.

I can remember working late in the garden on summer

afternoons, surrounded by clouds of gnats, hot as hell, my arms and back aching, and thinking, *Wow, is this great, or what?* Then I would think back to how unsatisfied I'd usually felt before as an adult. My next thought was: *Alice, you sly, patient dog, you've wormed your way in, haven't you?*

The Original Twelve Steps of Alcoholics Anonymous

1. We admitted we were powerless over alcohol—that our lives had become unmanageable.

2. Came to believe that a Power greater than ourselves could restore us to sanity.

3. Made a decision to turn our will and our lives over to the care of God as we understood Him.

4. Made a searching and fearless moral inventory of ourselves.

5. Admitted to God, to ourselves, and to another human being the exact nature of our wrongs.

6. Were entirely ready to have God remove all these defects of character.

7. Humbly asked Him to remove our shortcomings.

8. Made a list of all persons we had harmed and became willing to make amends to them all.

9. Made direct amends to such people wherever possible, except when to do so would injure them or others.

10. Continued to take personal inventory and when we were wrong promptly admitted it.

11. Sought through prayer and meditation to improve our conscious contact with God, as we understood Him, praying only for knowledge of His will for us and the power to carry that out.

12. Having had a spiritual awakening as the result of these Steps, we tried to carry this message to alcoholics, and to practice these principles in all our affairs.

About the Author

Martha Woodroof was born in the South, went to boarding school and college in New England, lived in Texas for a while, then fetched up in Virginia, where she's been ever since. She co-owned a couple of Charlottesville restaurants built around her cooking, then turned to broadcasting, finding true professional love in public radio. Her ambition is to do a good job telling other people's stories, and her work can be heard nationally on National Public Radio, Marketplace, and Weekend America.

Martha Woodroof lives with her husband in the Shenandoah Valley. Their closest neighbors are cows.

Thank you for reading *How to Stop Screwing Up*. Hampton Roads is proud to publish an extensive array of books on topics such as recovery, self-help, personal transformation, spirituality, and more. Please take a look at the following selection or visit us anytime on the web: www.hrpub.com.

Excuse Me, Your Life Is Waiting
The Astonishing Power of Feelings
Lynn Grabhorn

Ready to get what you want? Get this, hard work and positive thinking can't do it alone. Lynn Grabhorn introduces you to "The Law of Attraction" and uncovers the hidden power of positive feeling. Now in paperback, this upbeat yet down-to-earth book reveals how our true feelings work to "magnetize" and create the reality we experience. Discover the secrets that have made *Excuse Me* a **New York Times** bestseller!

Paperback • 328 pages • ISBN 978-1-57174-381-7 • $16.95

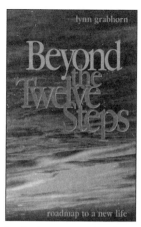

Beyond the Twelve Steps
Roadmap to a New Life
Lynn Grabhorn

What will it take for us to stop living dreary lives? What will it take for us to fill the deep ache and longing we all have for that elusive "something more"? Every bit as dynamic as *Excuse Me*, Lynn's first book is a courageous departure from the traditional twelve-step views of spirituality. Lynn takes our hungry souls on a life-changing journey to the kingdom within, laying out a path of startling new concepts to reconnect us with our own divinity.

Paperback • 240 pages • ISBN 978-1-57174-267-4 • $14.95

Excuse Me, Your Life Is Now
Doreen Banaszak

Lynn Grabhorn's wildly popular book, *Excuse Me, Your Life Is Waiting,* offered four fundamental principles for attracting what we desire most in life. Now Doreen Banaszak has created a sequel that not only presents a convenient review of Grabhorn's four basic tenets, but also offers overwhelming evidence, including dozens of first-person accounts, that these principles really work!

Paperback • 208 pages • ISBN 978-1-57174-543-9 • $15.95
Available August 2007

The Road to Power
Taking Control of Your Life
Barbara Berger

In this highly practical book, Berger offers the tools and then guides you, step by step, into how you can change your life by changing your thinking. If your life is not working, or you just want it to work better, here's a simple yet effective way to look inside yourself and see what you can do about money, relationships, love, your health, family, work, peace, joy, and much more.

Paperback • 208 pages • ISBN 978-1-57174-443-2 • $14.95

BeliefWorks
The Art of Living Your Dreams
Ray Dodd

Dodd offers a practical guide to understanding and reprogramming the core beliefs that drive your day-to-day decision making. Dodd reveals how our beliefs are constructed and then gives solutions for transforming the self-limiting beliefs that are holding you back.

Paperback • 200 pages
ISBN 978-1-57174-472-2 • $14.95

"When you change what you believe, you change your story about yourself, and suddenly life becomes a beautiful dream. *BeliefWorks* will show you how."

—don Miguel Ruiz, M.D., best-selling author of *The Four Agreements*

The Power of Belief
Essential Tools for an Extraordinary Life
Ray Dodd

Continuing in the tradition of the best-selling *The Four Agreements*, *The Power of Belief* reveals how our hidden beliefs create barriers to success and true happiness. An inspiring guide based on everyday wisdom, personal life coach Ray Dodd outlines four simple steps you can take to recreate any belief that stands in your way.

Paperback • 152 pages • ISBN 978-1-57174-404-3 • $14.95

The Beethoven Factor
The New Positive Psychology of Hardiness, Happiness, Healing, and Hope
Paul Pearsall, Ph.D., best-selling author of *The Pleasure Prescription* and *The Heart's Code*

This introduction to Positive Psychology, shows how to convert stress into personal discovery and transformation. At the book's core is Pearsall's work with "thrivers," those individuals who face life's challenges head-on and grow stronger and more vital as a result. *The Beethoven Factor* shows that you have the innate ability not only to weather life's storm but to tap into your "thriveability" and become better than ever before.

Hardcover • 304 pages • ISBN 978-1-57174-397-8 • $22.95

Smile for No Good Reason

Lee L. Jampolsky, Ph.D.

Trying to change your life's circumstances without addressing your way of thinking is as ineffective as painting over rust—it will only look good until the rust breaks through again. This trade paperback release of *Smile for No Good Reason* shares the twelve principles of Attitudinal Healing, a movement designed to show us how to achieve lasting happiness without having to change our social status, religion, or income bracket.

Paperback • 252 pages • ISBN 978-1-57174-415-9 • $14.00

Moving On
Finding Happiness in a Changed World

Stuart Perrin

Moving On is a book of street-smart, soul-wise aphorisms for dealing with the countless life events that make the world seem "changed." Separation, divorce, job loss, illness, the loss of a loved one—all of these are personal situations in which we all need a little perspective and wisdom in order to move on.

Paperback • 224 pages • ISBN 978-1-57174-371-8 • $12.00

Hampton Roads Publishing Company

. . . for the evolving human spirit

HAMPTON ROADS PUBLISHING COMPANY publishes books on
a variety of subjects, including metaphysics, spirituality,
health, visionary fiction, and other related topics.

For a copy of our latest trade catalog, call toll-free,
800-766-8009, or send your name and address to:

HAMPTON ROADS PUBLISHING COMPANY, INC.
1125 STONEY RIDGE ROAD • CHARLOTTESVILLE, VA 22902
e-mail: hrpc@hrpub.com • www.hrpub.com